The Parent's Guide

Use TV to Your Child's Advantage

S0-DJF-268

"

Many parents are discouraged about the kinds of TV programs their children are watching. This book can help parents make TV viewing a more educational and creative experience for their children, regardless of what programs they watch. It also provides welcome guidance on how to teach children to be more discriminating TV viewers."

Senator Daniel Inouye (D-Hawaii),
Chairman of the Communications Subcommittee
of the Senate Commerce, Science,
and Transportation Committee.

The Parent's Guide

Use TV to Your Child's Advantage

Dorothy G. Singer, Ed.D.
Jerome L. Singer, Ph.D.
Diana M. Zuckerman, Ph.D.

ACROPOLIS BOOKS LTD.

Authorization to photocopy items for internal or personal use, or the internal or personal use of specific clients, is granted by Acropolis Books Ltd., provided that the base fee of $1.00 per copy, plus $.10 per page is paid directly to Copyright Clearance Center, 27 Congress Street, Salem, MA 01970. For those organizations that have been granted a photocopy license by CCC, a separate system of payment has been arranged. The fee code for users of the Transactional Reporting Service is: "ISBN 0-87491-964-9/90 $1.00 + .10"

ACROPOLIS BOOKS LTD.
11741 Bowman Green Dr.
Reston, VA 22090

Attention: Schools and Corporations
ACROPOLIS books are available at quantity discounts with bulk purchase for educational, business, or sales promotional use. For information, please write to: SPECIAL SALES DEPARTMENT, ACROPOLIS BOOKS LTD., 13950 Park Center Rd., Herndon, VA 22071.

Are there Acropolis Books you want but cannot find in your local stores?
You can get any Acropolis book title in print. Simply send title and retail price. Be sure to add postage and handling: $2.25 for orders up to $15.00; $3.00 for orders from $15.01 to $30.00; $3.75 for orders from $30.01 to $100.00; $4.50 for orders over $100.00. District of Columbia residents add applicable sales tax. Enclose check or money order only, no cash please, to:
 ACROPOLIS BOOKS LTD.
 11741 Bowman Green Dr.
 Reston, VA 22090

Library of Congress Cataloging-in-Publication Data
Singer, Dorothy G.
    A parent's guide : use TV to your child's advantage / Dorothy G. Singer. Jerome L. Singer, Diana M. Zuckerman.
      p. cm.
    Includes bibliographical references.
    ISBN 0-87491-964-9 : $9.95
    1. Television and children—United States.   I. Singer, Jerome L.
II. Zuckerman, Diana M.   III. Title.
HQ784.T4S537   1990
791.45'013—dc20   90-34758
                                             CIP

Cover illustration and book design by Penny Kriese.

We dedicate this book to
The Singer grandchildren and to
Nicole Zuckerman Dubowitz

C O N T E N T S

Television has become increasingly important in children's lives. The average elementary school-aged child spends as much time watching television each day (five hours) as he or she spends in school. Even though some children devote considerably less time to watching TV, the time they do spend is time they will not be using for reading books, playing with friends, pursuing hobbies, talking with family members, and other important activities.

Television is here to stay, and although parents sometimes worry about their children's viewing habits, most parents feel unable or unwilling to limit children's television viewing. The purpose of this book is to encourage parents to use television programs to stimulate their children's learning and creativity, and to help parents to influence their children to be more selective television consumers. The activities presented are designed to be used with the TV programs that the children are already watching, and to make sure that the children under-stand program content as well as the differences between reality and fantasy on television. In addition, children's natural interest in television programs may be used as a motivating factor to foster critical thinking, reading and writing skills, and to encourage creativity.

This book is not intended to increase children's television viewing, but instead to help children get the most out of the programs they are already watching. Our intent is to stimulate more active participation between parent and child, and to counteract the passive TV-viewing syndrome. We also offer guidelines for parents who want to limit a child's viewing, and who want to help their children develop better television-viewing habits.

We want to thank our staff at the Yale University Family Television and Consultation Center for their devotion and skill in developing the materials, and especially Virginia Hurd for the excellent job in typing the manuscript and for helping us keep our balance. Thanks to Bruce Singer for his comments and suggestions. Lynne Shaner provided valuable editorial assistance.

Finally, we thank the school children, parents and teachers in Orange, Wilton and Stamford, Connecticut; Phoenix, Arizona; Cary, North Carolina; Lafayette, Indiana; Brookfield and Deerfield, Wisconsin; Valley Center and Santa Rosa, California; Omaha, Nebraska and Portland, Oregon who participated in trying out the exercises in this book.

Dorothy G. Singer, Ed.D., Jerome L. Singer, Ph.D.
Co-Directors Yale University Family Television
Research and Consultation Center
New Haven, CT
Diana M. Zuckerman, Ph.D., Professional Staff Member
Subcommittee on Human Resources and
Intergovernmental Relations, U.S. House of
Representatives

CHAPTER ONE

The Challenges of Television

Children today are growing up in an environment that never existed before about 1949 in human experience. In addition to family, friends, and the sights, smells, and noises of their homes, children today grow up with a little box which provides them with a vast array of sights and sounds far beyond their ordinary experience. They see funny cartoon animals falling apart and being miraculously put together, gangsters shooting down their victims with machine guns, cars pursuing each other down narrow roads, chorus girls kicking up their legs, all amid incessant interruptions by commercials in which humorous and lively figures dangle attractive candy bars or toys in front of children's eyes. That was a long sentence, but we used it on purpose. We wanted to capture the quality of the experience of a child who begins looking at the television set somewhere between one and two years of age and then continues watching it daily for as much as four or five hours as he or she grows up.

The evidence is pretty clear on the child's exposure to television. More than 99 percent of American families own at least one television set; many own two or three and 68.8 percent of households owned a videotape recorder at the end of 1989. In a certain sense, then, the television set can be viewed as "a member of the family." It is a major source of input of verbal and visual stimulation for the growing child, and we must take serious account of its impact.

Aside from the obvious characteristics of television—its availability in the home, its use of picture and sound, and its entertainment, information, and social value—television has certain properties that distinguish it from other communication media. They are:

- *Attention demand*—the continuous movement on the screen that evokes first an "orienting response" (focused attention), and then as movements become rapid and music louder, a general activation of the nervous system.

- *Brevity of sequences*—the brief interactions among people, vivid but short portrayals of events and rapidly-paced commercials (from 15 to 60 seconds long).

- *Interference effects*—the rapid succession of material that possibly interferes with the child's need to repeat mentally or to reflect upon and to assimilate new material.

- *Complexity of presentation*—the presentation of material to several senses at once—sight, sound, and printed words, especially in the commercials.

- *Visual orientation*—television is by its very nature concrete, oriented toward visual imagery, minimizing detailed attention to the other sources of input of information.

- *Emotional range*—the vividness of the action presented is greater than on other media.

In addition to these features there are the use of slow motion or speeded motion, split-screen techniques whereby two pictures are placed side by side on the same screen, the use of nearly subliminal techniques which allow two scenes to be viewed simultaneously (often used in dream sequences), and special camera effects such as zooming in (the enlargement of a character or object), making objects appear small or making them gradually grow before your eyes, the production of magical effects involving distortions, ripple effects of words or scenes, and, of course, the use of lighting and background music to create illusion. We are just beginning to see research appearing on whether these effects enhance or confuse a child's imagination and capacity to understand.

Problems Presented by the Television

Consider the problem, then, of understanding what is going on in the young child's mind. Miniature figures dance about on the screen; characters make statements which are quickly interrupted by new characters or changes in time or location. These rapid changes undoubtedly hold the child's attention on the screen, but they may do so at the cost of allowing the child an opportunity to *process* this material effectively. In other words, when subjected to very rapid presentations of novel material, the child lacks the time to replay this material mentally, to store it, and then to retrieve it efficiently at a later date.

The situation is not unlike one you might recognize yourself: coming into a party where the host introduces you rapidly to a whole series of people whom you have never met before. Naturally enough, you remember few names, if any. Television has a similar impact on young children. Its very liveliness holds their attention, arouses them, and may make them laugh, but they may have trouble remembering much of what they have seen afterward. There is a real danger that the rapidity of presentation may create "mindless" watching, so that by the end of the program there is little genuine comprehension of what has been watched, and often scarcely any memory.

We don't wish to minimize the importance television may have for some children and adults as a distraction. We often watch it to avoid thinking about the many pressing unfinished tasks of our daily life. Old people certainly find that it provides them with "company" to help them deal with loneliness.

At first one might think that television, with so much new vocabulary and so many new sights being presented to the child, would be on the whole an enriching experience. We must remember, however, that children are not miniature adults. When they watch a television program, they are comprehending the material on a different level from their parents. Children below the age of seven view the world illogically. They have difficulty separating reality from fantasy; they believe that inanimate objects, such as a teddy bear, can talk. They believe that human beings created lakes, mountains, sun, moon; they believe in magical thinking, and through their chants of "rain, rain go away" hope to control the elements. Their concepts of space and time are distorted. For example, a young child may believe that someone who lives 300 miles away is actually closer than someone who lives 60 miles away. If the trip to the farther point is made by plane, it is *shorter* in time than the trip to the nearer point when one travels by car. Young children believe taller people are *older* than shorter people. Children in the pre-operational stage think concretely; therefore metaphors and similes are difficult for them to understand. Words have literal meanings for them—the North

Pole is a long stick; "tied up at work" conjures up a picture of Daddy tied to his chair; and the phrase "he's lost his marbles" might make a youngster search on the floor. Children listen to words spoken on television, but they may be confused, misinterpret meanings, or perhaps even become frightened or upset at what they hear.

Certainly it is true that television creates a uniformity of experience across grossly different cultural groups within the country and, indeed, internationally. Almost everyone in America now knows how to sing the McDonald's hamburger jingle. To what extent, however, is the heavy visual emphasis of the medium affecting growing girls and boys? Important research by Sandra Witelson of McMaster University in Hamilton, Ontario suggests that girls are less differentiated than boys in right- and left-brain functioning. This means that they can use more of their brain for dealing with both verbal and spatial, or imagery material. Educators know that boys in the first seven or eight years of life are much more likely to have language difficulties than girls; the ratio is almost ten to one. The fact is that boys are heavier television viewers than girls and are thus more exposed to visually oriented material in which the verbal component is presented at extremely rapid rates. It is quite possible that this heavy visual emphasis creates further difficulties for a boy's ability to label verbally the images that are presented. In our own research we found advantages for girls in kindergarten in language usage, even though they watched as much television as boys.

It is also apparent from various research studies that children who watch a great deal of television are not engaging in conversation, an important part of how one learns to use language effectively. In one study, Eva Essa of Utah State University found that kindergarten-aged children, even when they were watching with their mothers, did not engage in much talk with their parents and simply regarded the set passively. Children who were heavy viewers did not show much play at other times, while children who were light viewers showed much more general interaction with their mothers and also more play with toys. In other research, Elizabeth Susman of Pennsylvania State University found that some of the special effects, such as zooming of the camera, tended to interfere with children's capacity to attend to the nature of the material being presented. Although for adults this so-called zoom effect may certainly focus attention, kindergarten-aged children are not able to benefit from this special effect and seem to be confused by it.

Unusual circumstances in Canada made it possible to compare three cities in which there were drastic differences in the availability of television. In one city, television had just been introduced for the first time. Linda Harrison of the University of British Columbia who carried out research on these cities, found that children, once having been exposed to television for a period of at least two years, did more poorly on a test where they were asked to name as many possible uses for common objects as they could. This drop indicated less creativity or original thinking by children who had now been watching TV regularly compared with the pre-television level.

The general trend of recent research seems to suggest that television may cause difficulties for children in developing the more active aspects of memory, in fostering better communication with parents (which enhances language use), and in developing an attitude of playfulness and imaginativeness. In an important project Robert Hornik of the University of Pennsylvania studied groups of children in El Salvador who were for the first time being exposed to television. He found strong evidence that reading improvement was *slowest* in children who now had a TV set, and that there was even some evidence that television interfered with general learning and reading ability. Here the simple distracting quality of the television set, interfering with the amount of time necessary to practice reading, was undoubtedly a factor. In our own research we found that children who were heavy TV viewers, and particularly viewers of "action" shows, had special difficulty in language development and in imaginative play. These children were also more aggressive and more likely to have difficulties in their day-to-day behavior in kindergarten.

In a more recent study with over 200 working-class families, we found that very frequent "Sesame Street" viewers tended to be among our most aggressive children in the nursery schools. It is possible that the fast pacing and short segments, ranging from about ten seconds to a minute and a half, may have been causing an arousal effect, and that the children's inability to process all the material properly causes their restlessness and increased likelihood of aggressive behavior in their play.

Another experimental study we carried out compared the effect of watching a slow-paced show, "Mister Rogers' Neighborhood," with that of watching the relatively rapid-paced children's show, "Sesame Street." While the brighter young girls were able to learn more of the material seen on "Sesame Street," it turned out that the less intelligent boys and less imaginative children did somewhat better with the slower-paced "Mister Rogers'." In his book, *"Sesame Street" Revisited,* Thomas D. Cook and his colleagues reported that middle-class children actually learned more from "Sesame Street" than lower-class children, because they were encouraged to watch the program by their parents. These parents may also have been more active in reinforcing ideas from "Sesame Street" with their children than parents in lower socioeconomic groups. If we are to avoid increasing the knowledge gap across social classes, we must provide as wide a variety of television formats as possible so that children from all backgrounds can profit from viewing. We must also clearly encourage parents to interact with their children as they watch television.

There are two more problems about television viewing that we should like to mention. One is the fact that in general the pacing of programs may prevent children from practicing their own imagery and trying out in play and thought some of the new material observed. In effect, the TV format trains one simply to watch the set and to be satisfied with that.

We found in our own research that with the "Mister Rogers' Neighborhood" program, in which great emphasis was placed on repetition of words, on careful phrasing, on encouragement of imagination and the child's "talking back" to the set, children were able to play more imaginatively than when they watched other kinds of television fare. Having an adult available who would encourage imaginativeness was also important.

Television, according to psychologist W. Andrew Collins, has also created difficulties for kindergartners in understanding causal sequences. That is, children who saw aggressive acts could rarely understand whether the act was motivated by good or bad intentions. They simply remembered the aggression. There is increasing evidence from a variety of research studies which suggests that the excitement of the aggression is imitated in many different ways by the children. Our own research suggests that kindergarten children who had displayed aggressive behavior for over a year were also more likely to have watched programs with arousing content, such as game shows in which the winners leap up and down screaming hysterically.

Some final points. Television presents continuous movement. It is a medium that is controlled by others. Information flashes by and the child cannot go back over it. There is no sense of control over the medium except to shut it off. Currently, there is the widespread availability of videocassettes which give the viewer at least some sense of input into what appears on the screen. Television, however, is not like reading, where one has the possibility of self-pacing. With a book, one can read the text again and again until the material is grasped more firmly. To some degree one has a sense of control over the reading process. At the same time there exists the possibility of stopping, of elaborating more fully upon one's visual or auditory images in connection with the material, and thus increasing the possibility of storing the materials in the brain in an efficient fashion. Clearly this is a very distinct process from what goes on in the television-viewing situation.

It might seem unlikely that one can develop imagery as vivid and rich from reading as one can from the immediacy of a television presentation. Nevertheless, the images that have been developed while reading have been *worked at* and are more clearly one's own. This is why people who have first "read the book" are so often disappointed by the movie. Since reading is a basic skill for effective functioning in our modern society, we have to be concerned about the possibility that heavy television viewing, and particularly viewing under circumstances which may preclude the development of imagination, may also interfere with the child's development of reading skills.

It may sound as if television is an enemy and that we are sounding a call to arms for the abolition of television. In one of our research studies we attempted to train parents to control and severely limit children's TV viewing. This turned out to be very difficult to do. Parents like television themselves, and they also find it an extremely convenient baby-sitter. In fact, parents from the poorer inner-city neighborhoods often say that they would rather have their children home watching television than out in the streets confronting various dangers. Rather than abolish television, we should find ways of harnessing its tremendous power in the direction of more effective education for children.

In the United States there are very few programs available to kindergarten-aged children or even children below the age of twelve that are seriously designed to be both entertaining and educational, promoting intellectual growth and also a sense of cooperation and positive social attitudes. We would like to see television producers provide more of such programs, with pacing that is appropriate for children to comprehend and with much more conscious effort to communicate directly with the younger children. The television medium can be a great advantage for the growing child and a stimulant for imagination if material is presented in a format that is suitable for the child. Our activities make a special point of encouraging imaginativeness and, for older children, include exercises that involve practice in reading and writing with ideas drawn from television.

Ultimately, of course, the adults in the child's life have the most to contribute in stimulating the child's imagination and encouraging an atmosphere that will lead on the one hand to a willingness and interest in reading, and on the other to a discriminating and moderate approach to television viewing. One of our favorite images of the joys of child-rearing is the scene of the father or mother or grandparent telling a tale or reading from a book to a wide-eyed, eager child. Certainly, no electronic device can ever substitute for the warmth of interchange between a loving adult and a child at storytelling time; nevertheless, in the following chapters we hope to show that television can be used creatively toward constructive ends.

Constructive Possibilities and Hazards of Television

Sol Levine of Highland Park, Illinois, estimates that he is saving the nation one barrel of crude oil a year by having his children pedal a bike-generator he invented to power their television set.

> "I'd come home and find my two kids immobilized in front of their set and I figured they should be doing something if they wanted to watch it," says Levine, president of an ecology center for saving energy. "I took their bicycle, made a stand for it in the TV room, hooked it to a car generator and a 12-volt battery. Now they can feed their television habit with their own energy." Levine says the pedal power can work only on a set about the size used by Bennet, 15, and Linda, 12—a black-and-white portable with a 12-inch screen. "I pedal with them sometimes to watch the late news," Levine says. "It's good exercise. My wife used to join us pedaling through programs, but now she regards it mainly as exercise. When the kids are at school,

she will do some pedaling in the afternoon and help charge the battery."

On a busy TV night, Levine and the children take turns pedaling, storing electricity for five-minute recesses. "We usually take a break during commercials."

—Quoted in *New York Newsday*

Mr. Levine is one parent who is aware of television's power over his children. The average number of hours spent viewing television varies from about 3 hours a day for preschoolers to 5 hours a day for elementary school-aged children. We also know that poor and black children spend even more time—approximately 5½ to 6 hours per day—before the television set. In our own studies at the Yale Family Television Research and Consultation Center, we have found that both middle-class and lower-class children between three and five average about 22 to 23 hours per week, and for our middle-class sample of more than 100 children the range of viewing per week was from 1 to 72 hours. Obviously, television is playing a major role in children's lives; for a large segment of the school-aged population, more time is spent in front of the screen than in school.

Our studies (one begun in 1976, with a sample of 140 middle-class children, and a study with 200 working-class families that we completed in 1980) support findings concerning the deleterious effect of TV on children. Children who are heavy television viewers and who are the most aggressive in our samples watch action-detective shows, cartoons, news, and game shows. We find that both the hours spent in front of television and program content are significant. For example, heavy viewers of educational programs do not exhibit as much aggressive behavior as viewers of action-detective shows.

In addition to the television viewing patterns of children, family interaction and behavior also influence a child's capacity for aggression. We found that an aggressive child is more likely to be part of a family that uses television as its main socializing force. Family members spend little time visiting zoos, parks, libraries, or even relatives. The focus of entertainment is television. Meals are even eaten in front of the set, inhibiting communication. Thus, there is little to protect the child against the powerful effect of the television characters or of the special properties of the medium—especially those who present models for aggression and violence. The most shocking finding is that in these homes the child very often controls the set and stays up late watching TV with other family members.

Teaching Elementary School Children to Become Critical Consumers of Television

The project most important to this book is a study we designed to teach elementary school children how to be more discriminating television viewers. We developed an eight-lesson curriculum in 1980 that was tested for four weeks in two schools in Orange, Connecticut, a suburb of New Haven. Each lesson reviewed an aspect of television aimed at increasing children's understanding of TV and developing a more critical approach to TV viewing.

The major goals of the lessons were as follows:

1. To identify the different types of programs, such as news, documentaries, variety, game shows, situation comedies, and drama.

2. To understand that programs are created by writers, producers, and directors, and that shows utilize trained

actors and actresses, as well as carefully constructed scenery and props.

3. To understand in simple form something of the electronics of television.

4. To learn what aspects of a program are "real," and how fantasy is created on programs or commercials by using camera techniques and special effects.

5. To learn about commercials, their purpose, what kinds there are, as well as about public service or political announcements.

6. To understand how television influences our feelings, ideas, self-concepts, and identification.

7. To become aware of television as a source of information about other people, countries, and occupations, and how stereotypes are often presented.

8. To examine violence on television with a view toward removing its false glamour. To become aware that we rarely see someone recovering from an act of violence on TV, see the aggressor punished, or are shown the many non-aggressive means of resolving conflicts.

9. To encourage children to be aware of what they watch and how they can control their viewing habits, and of how they can influence networks, producers, and local TV stations.

10. To use these lessons within a language arts curriculum so that children could gain experience for using correct grammar and spelling, for writing letters, for abstracting ideas, engaging in critical thinking, and for using language effectively through oral discussion and in reading.

We designed each lesson to run about 40 to 50 minutes. Included were activities for classroom and homework, and the lessons encompassed reading, writing, and critical-thinking skills.

The teacher introduced the lesson using a discussion guide that we had prepared. For example, in dealing with the lesson on violence and aggression, the children were asked to name any show they had seen the previous week that had aggression in it. These were listed on the blackboard. Children were asked to define aggression and to make distinctions between physical and verbal aggression. They talked about the difference between aggression and assertiveness, and the meaning of violence. A ten-minute videotape was shown, followed by discussion exploring the causes and effects of violent acts. Did they see the victim suffer? Did they see punishment meted out on the TV screen? Teachers asked whether or not anyone had ever imitated an aggressive act following a show. In one homework assignment, for example, children were asked to keep track of aggressive acts in a cartoon or dramatic program that they had recently watched. All lessons followed a discussion-activity format.

In order to evaluate whether the children learned what they had been taught in the lessons, we tested them before and after the four-week curriculum. We compared their test scores with those of children in another school who took the same tests but did not receive the curriculum that we developed.

Our comparisons of the test scores demonstrated that children made gains in defining lesson-related words such as *audio, fiction, prop,* and *aggression.* They also learned to identify videotaped examples of special effects, and to describe how camera techniques and effects distort reality in programs and commercials. In addition, they learned to differentiate between real people, realistic characters, and fantasy characters. Three months after the lessons were completed, the children still remembered the information they had learned. Children were also able to answer questions relating to examples *not* previously taught in the lessons.

Television Viewing Habits and Family Background

We also wanted to learn more about the relationship between children's TV viewing and aspects of family life. We found that the parents' viewing habits were the most important predictors of their children's. Children who spent more time watching television tended to have parents who were heavy television viewers, and were less likely to have parentally imposed limits on their TV viewing. This finding appears again in studies we carried out in the mid 1980s.

Television Viewing Habits and Teacher Ratings

We were also interested to learn more about the association between children's viewing habits and their behavior in school. Teachers evaluated the children's aggressiveness, cooperation, attentiveness, interpersonal relationships, enthusiasm, happiness, and imagination. The viewing pattern most important in predicting classroom behavior was watching fantasy-violent programs. Teachers described children who (unknown to the teachers) watched more fantasy-violent programs as less cooperative, less successful in their relationships, less happy, and less imaginative, regardless of the children's IQ scores. Teachers rated the children whom our data showed had watched more cartoons as unenthusiastic about learning. Aggressive behavior and attentiveness in class were not related to television viewing in this study but in other research we did find that heavy viewers were more restless and also showed more behavior problems in school.

Television Viewing, Reading, and IQ

One of the most controversial issues in education is the concern about television and reading. Will heavy television viewing affect a child's ability to read? We are aware that children learn to read by *practicing* reading each day, and we were curious about television's encroachment on reading time. We examined the reading and IQ scores of the children in this study, as well as the teachers' and parents' estimates of their children's reading habits, in order to determine the relationship between television viewing and reading.

The children in this study watched television about 15 hours per week and are rather atypical viewers compared to the national norms of 20 to 30 hours per week for children in this age group. The children are also above average in terms of IQ and reading ability, with an average IQ of 110 and a reading score approximately one year above grade level.

Teachers kept track of the number of books the children read during a four-week period, and even when we took into account the differences in intelligence and grade level, the children who read more books were the ones who also watched fewer game shows and variety programs. Children who spent more time reading had higher IQ's and more highly educated fathers, and watched fewer fantasy-violent programs. It may be that children who read well, and therefore enjoy fantasy and escape through reading, rely less on television to fulfill this need. On the other hand, the poorer reader may seek adventure and action by turning to television as a source.

Television Viewing, and Racial and Sex Prejudice

As a part of the study, we attempted to determine whether or not television viewing was related to prejudice. We found that girls who watched more game or variety programs and reruns that present women as silly or incompetent (such as "I Love Lucy" and "The Jetsons") were more prejudiced against girls than their classmates were. In contrast, the girls who watched more fantasy-violent programs and *fewer* other violent programs were less prejudiced against girls. The female role models in fantasy-violent programs are often competent and beautiful (e.g., "Wonder Woman") and are *not* the victims who are usually found in the more "realistic" action-detective shows. Boys' sex prejudice was not related to their television habits.

Children who were the most prejudiced against black children were those who watched more violent programs (where blacks are often portrayed in negative ways). They watched *fewer* programs with major black characters where blacks are portrayed more favorably.

Television Viewing, Hobbies, and Other Activities

Our last analysis looked at the relationship between children's TV-viewing habits and their other activities. We wanted to learn whether children who watch more television are less involved in playing with friends, pursuing hobbies, engaging in athletics, or doing things with other family members. We asked parents to describe the kinds of activities that their children regularly participated in, and asked them to estimate the amount of time they spent in these activities each week.

The children who spent the most time watching TV each week also were involved in family activities (including watching TV together) and in music and dancing. However, these children were less likely to read with their parents.

The children who were heavy viewers of violent television programs played less with friends. We don't know if this is because these children do not get along well with other children or if it is because they prefer activities such as watching violent programs to games with friends. The children who watched more fantasy-violent programs spent less time on hobbies and less time doing homework with their parents' help.

We were also interested in children's viewing of cartoons, situation comedies, and dramas. In each case the children who were watching TV the most were those who had fewer hobbies, played less with friends, and were less involved with athletics, religious activities, and/or music lessons. In contrast, the children who watched more sports programs spent *more* time on athletic activities.

These results can't tell us which comes first: Does TV viewing replace other activities, or do other activities limit the amount of time children have left for TV? In either case the results suggest that children who watch less TV tend to have more interest and participate in more activities where they can learn to get along with other children, as well as family members.

This study suggests that television has a place in the classroom as well as in the home if it is used with discretion. The dramatic impact of a story viewed by a group of students creates a shared emotional experience that could lead to fruitful discussion and changes in attitudes.

The use of television for cognitive, social and emotional benefits is still in the pioneering stage. Certainly, whatever a child is exposed to for several hours on a daily basis is bound to have effects. On television, children see a wide array of human emotions, sexual encounters, violence, and aggression. Many children watch programs alone, and even those who watch with adults do not process the messages in the same way as adults. They are left with misunderstandings and confusion, and they are often frightened by the content. Moreover, using a simple questionnaire, we found that heavy television viewers *of all ages* are more frightened by the world around them and judge it to be a "scary" place.

We found, too, that children whose families impose no limits on viewing, and whose mothers watch a great deal of TV, exhibit poorer comprehension of plots and show greater confusion between reality and fantasy. Despite all their hours of viewing, these children have a poorer acquisition of general information than do children in families that limit TV viewing.

As a result of these outcomes, we began to look at what we called *mediation*—those behaviors that pertain to parent-child communication in general and to television viewing in particular. How does family mediation shape a child's view of the world? Can family mediation modify the outcomes of television viewing as a child matures?

We discovered that two important components are involved in the mediation process: *control/discipline* and *communication*. Control/discipline refers to physical punishment, forceful verbal displays, or love-withdrawal methods (expressions of disappointment and concomitant denial of verbal and physical affection). Communication refers to answering a child's questions; providing spontaneous explanations about people, entities, or events; or sharing critical, evaluative comments about the child or a particular situation. Communication also implies parental efforts geared toward reinforcing the child's desirable speech and actions.

Generally, we have found that power-assertive methods of discipline are linked to aggressive behavior in children and are frequently employed with more aggressive boys. Love-withdrawal modes of discipline are more frequently used with girls, but less is known about the later developmental consequences of this style of mediation. Helen Block Lewis, a leading expert in shame and guilt, believed that love-withdrawal discipline probably contributes to the heavy role of shame in women more than in men.

In the fall of 1983, we began a three-year study of 91 kindergartners and first graders in the metropolitan area of New Haven, Connecticut, to learn how different families used mediation in relation to television viewing. We gathered information on parental attitudes toward discipline and child rearing, general mediation styles, parental beliefs about safety and stress, amount and kind of television viewed by parents and children, and parents' and children's reports of television-specific mediation in the home. The children were studied at school and during visits to the research center at Yale University, and in the third year, a subsample was observed at home over several three-hour time periods.

We were interested in seeing how mothers responded to their children in a variety of daily life situations such as shopping, visiting the doctor, riding in an automobile, and so on. Mothers' responses were scored for such categories as making moral judgments, pointing things out, giving explanations, providing discipline, engaging the children's participation in decision making, and preparing the child for novel situations before or after they were confronted.

We found that parents tended to deal with their children in one of two basic ways: through *discussion* or through *prescription*. Parents using discussion engaged in anticipatory or after the fact explanations of events in the child's life. Parents using prescription stifled discussions with such commands as "Stop it," "Be quiet," or "Leave me alone!" We anticipated that a family member who emphasized discussion would be the sort of person who could help a child to differentiate and organize his or her environment, to understand and retain new information, and to form new ideas or plans. Such a person could use discussion to help the child comprehend television material and adapt a more critical attitude toward the programs viewed.

More specifically, we were interested in learning how parents used rules concerning television viewing hours and whether specific programs were discouraged or forbidden. Our analysis of the data reveals that a particular family style correlates with the child's acquisition of *greater* general information and *less* aggression or motor restlessness. This style involves parents who establish television rules, a mother who is perceived (by the child) as making positive comments, and parents who engage in *active* discussion with their children and in controlled television use, less television viewing, and less power assertion.

Our analysis also reveals additional findings. For one, it is clear that unrestricted exposure to television does *not* teach children to be more discriminating viewers. Nor does it help them acquire general knowledge or a better grasp of plots, commercials, or special effects (such as zoom photography). On the other hand, parental involvement—in the form of explanation, discussion, and critical comments about negative or hostile acts portrayed on television—has a powerful mitigating effect on television's influence on a child's development. Another interesting finding is that a parental style involving *prescription* rather than *discussion,* and including a frequent pattern of negative comments by the mother, is associated with greater fear of an "unjust world" by the child.

An important point that emerges from this study is that "love is not enough." Positive family communication patterns *alone* do not produce children with the best comprehension and reading scores. A combination of *control* over hours and programs viewed and *explanation and commentary* on the programming is the most powerful weapon we have to combat this television dilemma.

A great deal of emphasis has been placed on the negative effects of television. It's time now for educators and researchers to find ways to use this powerful medium more creatively and to influence people to help and respect each other.

CHAPTER THREE

Parents' Questions About TV

Over the past twenty years we have become increasingly aware of parental concerns regarding television. When we speak at professional conferences or parent meetings, similar questions usually arise concerning the scheduling of appropriate programs for children, the influence of violence and aggression, the effects of cartoons and stereotypes, the effects on imagination and language, and finally the problem of what to do about commercials. In this chapter we will address those questions that are asked most frequently. Perhaps in reading this, you will recognize some of your own concerns, or indeed, you may become aware of some issues that you hadn't thought about previously.

Can Television-Viewing Affect Vision?

One of the more common concerns of parents is the possibility that television could be harmful to their children's eyes. The national Society for the Prevention of Blindness offers these suggestions for television viewing:

- Focus the TV so that the image is clear and distinct.
- The picture should be steady.
- The room should be properly lighted (not darkened), without too much contrast of light between the room and the screen. Soft, indirect lighting is best, with no light source reflected from the screen to the viewer's eyes.
- The screen should be viewed from a comfortable distance in front of the screen, (about 3 or 4 feet) not from an angle, and at eye level, not from the floor.
- Resting the eyes by looking away from the screen at frequent intervals is recommended.

Who Controls the TV Set?

Quarrels in many families revolve around the program scheduling and time limits. Generally speaking, children can accept family rules if they are consistently enforced by parents and if the children are given constructive alternatives. The parents must stick to their beliefs and limit late viewing or potentially disturbing shows. The pressure of school friends should not override parents' better judgment.

When a three-year-old prefers to watch "Sesame Street" and his eight-year-old brother wants to watch his favorite show, a problem is bound to arise as to who's "boss." The decision here is an important one, for what three-year-olds watch on TV should be determined by their parents and never by older brothers or sisters. Parents can make clear for the young child that there are certain times *each* child can watch TV, and regularly limit those times so young children will grow up expecting such restrictions.

At times a baby-sitter may want to watch a program that you feel is unsuitable for your child. Be careful to let the sitter know your rules, and that you expect him or her to abide by them. Sometimes your child visits a friend and watches a program of which you disapprove. You can't always be the supervisor, but hopefully, if your child truly understands your feelings about specific program viewing, he will most likely try to obey. Chances are that if you have been consistent, your child will establish viewing habits that you approve. In general, parents should always be aware of their responsibility to know how much time the children spend with the TV and what they are watching. Parents can't assume that another family will always show good judgment. Many families don't pay attention at all to the kinds of TV their children watch and are surprised when the children have nightmares or sleeping difficulties.

Should Children Watch TV During Meals or When Doing Homework?

Parents also ask if doing homework or eating meals in front of television is harmful. Most educators believe that even though children might get the homework done while watching TV, the division of attention prevents them from learning as effectively as when the television is turned off. Parents should establish a regular schedule to follow—an allotted time for homework and then a regular time for TV on the condition that all homework has been finished. As we pointed out earlier, watching TV reduces the amount of time available for reading and thinking imaginatively. A regular schedule should allow time when undivided attention can be given to reading practice. This increases the likelihood that the child will develop consistently good reading habits. Except for the occasional treat, eating in front of the TV set establishes a very bad habit.

It reinforces the children's dependence on TV, may lead to overeating, and breaks down family togetherness and communication. According to research, eating while watching programs will have an even worse effect of "hooking" children on TV. A sense of family structure would be better served by keeping very young children on regular early-bedtime schedules and helping their imaginations grow through reading, storytelling, or play. Older children can share activities with their parents in the evening by playing board games, working on hobbies, and sharing in music or sports activities.

What Kinds of TV Shows Should Children Watch?

There have been many questions asked about the effects of cartoons on children. We find in our research that heavy viewing of cartoons leads to inappropriate and disruptive behavior among children in nursery school. Among our elementary school-aged children, the heavy cartoon viewers were rated as "unenthusiastic about school" by their teacher. Even though some parents may enjoy sleeping late on Saturday morning and rely on television as a baby-sitter, we feel they should first become familiar with the shows presented on Saturday mornings and set rules about *what shows* and *how many* the children can watch.

All children's shows are not alike. Some cartoons involve considerable violence, which agitates children and makes them more likely to tend toward aggressive behavior. Other shows are very frightening in content. The parent should never allow the TV set to substitute for his or her judgment and should establish limits on frequency and content of cartoon viewing. Some parents claim that their children are quiet *only* when they watch TV; otherwise they are constantly active or getting into trouble. Thus, the parents particularly like Saturday morning, when the programs are geared to children. Most research, however, suggests that the very active child or the child who gets into fights becomes even more agitated by frequent TV viewing, especially when material involves cartoons, action-detective programs, or noisy game shows. There is no reason to believe that frequent viewing will quiet down a child. Hyperactive children need to learn to play imaginatively and to find resources in *themselves* rather than depending solely on their environment for stimulation. Parents should especially try to restrict such a child's television viewing to shows that they have prescreened and that involve interesting material but little violence. They should encourage such a child to play with other children and to play imaginative games or to work at constructing games out of blocks, Legos, etc.

Active children are also more prone to imitate the acrobatics they see on television. Following any broadcast of daring stunts, a surprising number of children in the United States will be injured trying to duplicate such feats on tricycles and bicycles. Even with parental explanation, young children may not grasp all that is involved in developing such skills. Older children are more aware of real dangers and are less inclined toward rash imitation. When such stunt events are broadcast, parents of preschoolers should take a firm stand in the family and simply watch an alternative show or plan another family event to avoid the temptation of viewing by the children.

Sometimes parents ask us if "soaps" are permissible programs for young children to view. Some mothers have stated that they enjoy these programs and watch them regularly as a relief from housework. They enjoy the company of their young children as they watch together, and yet have wondered if the content is harmful. We believe that neither parent nor child should watch television as a main entertainment source, but rather should try to find more active ways of relieving boredom. Parents should recognize how much children learn by imitation. If they can control their own TV viewing patterns and find more constructive things to do with children, they can avoid hooking children on TV. The material presented on soap operas is not always appropriate for young children and may simply be confusing or frightening to them. If parents *do* watch with their children, it is important to point out that these are *stories,* and may be exaggerations of problems that people face.

Some programs that elementary school-aged children watch contain violent acts, fairly explicit sex, and sometimes even rape. Parents have asked if they should laugh off these incidents, divert the children's attention from the screen by chatter or by offering food or snacks, or quickly jump up and turn off the set. We feel that a parent should try to explain that sometimes *some* people behave in this fashion. Use explanations that your children can grasp in terms of their age and ability to understand. It is difficult to always shield a child from exposure to some antisocial act that he may see on TV. Let the child know you are available to talk about it. It is always better to deal with the facts maturely than to deny the existence of aggression and sex.

One of the major concerns parents express about television is the effect of violent programs on their children. Research over the past two decades has demonstrated that television programs that have violent content lead to aggressive behavior in children, especially those who are heavy television viewers and who have little else in the way of a social life. In Chapter 10, we discuss this important issue more fully. We do suggest that parents restrain young children's viewing of violent programming.

Evidence strongly points to a relationship between the viewing of action-detective shows and aggression. We have also found that such noisy, fast-paced programs as game shows, cartoons, and some variety shows can arouse a child to aggression or jumpiness. Some parents are pleased that their children watch game shows because they feature quizzes on information and word matching. We feel that parents should restrict viewing to the less noisy shows with less screaming. Although potentially a child is exposed to lots of information from game shows, the noisy formats, rapid presentation, and emphasis on competition may prevent a child from really grasping and remembering very much. Instead, the child may be viewing the programs passively. Parents should encourage the child to write or rehearse the questions and answers and to share them. Some genuine learning may be possible, but parents cannot count on the TV to substitute for conversation and real family sharing of knowledge and skill. In fact, our research suggests that light television viewers use longer sentences, more adjectives and adverbs, and more varied tenses than heavy viewers.

What Kinds of Beliefs and Attitudes Can Children Pick up from TV?

Parents are often sensitive about programs that deal with special problems such as adoption, alcohol, drugs, and the handicapped child; yet often such programming can be used by parents to discuss these important and delicate issues with their children. Keeping a mature program off the air may impede discussions of significant, basic experiences.

Television can also offer a family an opportunity to discuss stereotypes. Many parents ask what they can do about the ways in which women, African-Americans, and old people are presented on television. Parents should remember that it is the discussion, not the viewing, that is important. For example, when commercials depict stereotyped pictures of women, parents can discuss these misrepresentations and suggest to their children that they should rely on their own experience for judging situations, rather than on television. You might want to say, "Remember those ads are just there to try to get you to buy certain products. They just show so many women cleaning or cooking to show off the products. In our house we all pitch in together to get the work done."

The presentation of families and family situations on television can also be misleading to children. Many real-life families are obviously not middle class, comfortable, and physically perfect, and parents must point out that the "ideal" families sometimes presented on television are simply not accurate representations of reality. In this respect television can be a springboard for intelligent and valuable discussions about family differences in income and life-style. Banning such viewing may simply give the material more importance than it deserves, and ignoring such influences may reinforce unrealistic hopes among children and also lead to envy or dissatisfaction with parents.

Children may pick up offensive language from TV. If parents watch programs with their children where characters are maligned or where offensive language is used, they can show how the audience is laughing at, not with, the offender. They can also point out that using offensive language can have very negative consequences.

Sometimes parents who are foreign-born have asked us what to say to their children, who point out that people on TV usually don't have accents. Parents can recognize the natural differences in speech. Here again, one can point up the wide range of differences among families in American society, and at the same time call attention to the limited representations on TV of the different ethnic groups.

What Can We Do about Commercials?

Finally, there is the question of commercials and their effects. When children beg for a toy because "everybody has one," it's important for a parent to convey to children a realistic picture of what a family can afford and also to point out how a commercial can mislead them. Adopting a completely negative approach, however, may simply evoke anger or frustration in the child, for children are captivated by ads, particularly those that display a "free prize," usually a plastic toy featured in an ad for a cereal. As parents know, children will generally use the toy once before breaking it or throwing it away, and may not even like the cereal. Parents should make sound decisions concerning young children's food choices and not be swayed by those "extras." Consistency will quickly teach the preschooler what your standards are. This can be done by explaining each situation firmly but kindly to the child. Merely attacking credibility of a famous person who is peddling a product, or putting down a product because it is expensive, a luxury, or just a waste may only confuse a child. A simple explanation as to why you are not going to buy the product is more constructive than an attack on either the product or the people selling it.

This sampling of the questions we are often asked could be used as a stimulus for family discussions. As you continue to read the book and carry out activities with your child, the information we present will help clarify any other problems or concerns we may have only touched here.

When You Watch and What You Watch

You're ready now to begin our "home minicourse" to help you and your child understand how television works and how it influences your thinking. We designed the activities that follow each chapter so that all you need is your TV set, some paper, and a pencil. We suggest that you become familiar with each chapter before you start to teach your child. It would be best to follow our order of presentation, but feel free to choose any lesson that you think is interesting or important to your family. Depending on your child's age, you may want to put our ideas into your own words, simplify some of the concepts, and choose the appropriate activities. You might want to do one lesson a week, or perhaps two, again depending upon your time and your child's ability, interest, and motivation. Check through the chapters before you begin. The exercises focus on television content, but the information and activities should stimulate learning and language arts skills such as vocabulary building and critical thinking. Remember that our approach is designed for elementary school aged children. For younger children or adolescents you can use this material as a basis for discussion. The earlier you start the better!

Helping Your Child to Watch TV Intelligently

Before we get to the television lessons, you might want to get a sense of how much television you and your children actually watch in a typical week. You should keep a record of the number of shows viewed each day and how long each member of the family watches them. Once you have this information, you can make some decisions about the amount of viewing you do: Is it too much? Is there one family member watching more than anyone else? Are you viewing any programs together? If so, how many? What kinds of programs are you watching? Is your child viewing television alone?

If your child is watching a great deal of television, you should impose some reasonable limits. Check out his or her other activities. Does your child have friends nearby? Does the family engage in any joint activities? Can you suggest a hobby or some games to play as a substitute? If your child is viewing television alone, have you prescreened the programs? Are they suitable for his or her age?

You should be aware if your child is *reading* less as a result of TV viewing. If your child is reading very little, you should suggest some books that are related to his or her favorite TV shows. There are many good books about sports, science fiction, cowboys, and fantasy that would motivate your child to read. "The Hardy Boys" and "Nancy Drew" series, for example, inspired many children to read, and "Little House on the Prairie" has been a library best seller since the TV series began.

What You Need to Know

The goal of this chapter is to help children develop an under-standing of the different types of programs that are on TV. Parents are usually unaware of the fact that even though children might be able to describe a show's content and remember the program's name, they may have no idea of the *type* of program it is. Children often don't even realize that different types of programs exist at all!

Children, like adults, have varied preferences for particular kinds of programs. Preschool children generally prefer cartoons, situation comedies, and noncartoon children's programs; first and second graders enjoy situation comedies; and eleven-and twelve-year-olds cite action-adventure shows as favorites (although by these ages children also enjoy watching music, variety, dramatic, and sports programs).

There are some sex differences in viewing patterns among children. Boys, for example, tend to watch more violent cartoons, western, crime, and action-adventure shows than girls. As boys grow older, they view more sports and public-affairs programs, while girls are more likely to watch situation comedies and some variety shows. Young children watch news programs only occasionally until adolescence, when they begin to watch the news on a more regular basis. In two of our studies, for example, we found that elementary school-aged children rarely watched educational programs on public television and clearly preferred situation comedies and fantasy-adventure shows. In laboratory observations, researchers found that boys are more attentive to cartoons than girls and are particularly attracted to commercials that contain incidents of action, violence, and special effects.

With the introduction of cable, movie channels, and videotape players, we find that television viewing increases. The electronic family, a family with cable, movie channels, videotape players, more than one television set, and several kinds of computer games, has the highest number of television viewing hours per week compared to families where such electronic equipment is minimal.

Parental choices and program availability determine children's exposure to adult programs. When children outgrow cartoons and "Sesame Street" and "Mister Rogers' Neighborhood," they prefer to watch comedies, the least demanding kind of program for a six- or seven-year-old to comprehend.

When children are asked why they watch television, similar results are found from a variety of studies. Escape from current problems is a major reason among young people. In addition, children find emotional satisfaction through identification with television characters. Television keeps children company; they gain knowledge and information; and it can be a substitute source for social contacts with other children.

Parents exert very little control over specific programs their children view. One study found that 92 percent of approximately 5000 parents of fourth through ninth graders provided no guidance on Saturday mornings, and on school nights 75 percent of these parents imposed *no* limitation on the amount of television their children watched.

Let's now review the different kinds of TV programs that are available. There are **adventure programs,** such as "Mac-Gyver," "Quantum Leap," "Paradise," and "Rescue 911." Some of these are more realistic than others. The events in "Rescue 911," for example, could happen in real life, while the adventures in "Quantum Leap" often use fantasy. **Cartoons** such as

"Smurfs," "Yogi Bear," "Jetsons" and "Superfriends" are make-believe and *animated*. To produce an animated effect, a camera photographs many hundreds of different drawings—each representing a different movement. When the drawings are all run together, the characters and objects seem to move.

Comedy programs such as "Alf," "Who's the Boss?," "Growing Pains," "Family Matters," and "The Cosby Show" are very popular with children. The characters are realistic; they do and say things that people in real life can do, but are created by the script writers. We also have nonviolent drama programs on television, such as "Life Goes On," and "Young Riders." There are funny moments on these shows, but usually the characters are dealing with more serious matters. These programs have touched on problems that many families face, such as serious illness, concern with finances, problems with school or friends, birth of babies, and even death. Most of the people on these programs are also realistic, and, like characters in comedy shows, are made up by the writer.

Sometimes television networks present **education programs** such as "Animals, Animals, Animals" and "The Electric Company" (to help children read and learn numbers); "Jacques Cousteau" (specials about life underwater); "3–2–1 Contact," (a program to teach children about science); and programs for preschoolers, such as "Mister Rogers' Neighborhood" and "Sesame Street." There are also game shows (such as "Wheel of Fortune," "Family Feud," and "Jeopardy!") which award contestants prizes or money if they answer various questions correctly.

Serials, or **soap operas,** are dramatic presentations of a continuing story. The plots of these shows are varied, with many interrelated subplots and side stories. Many of the conflicts and mysteries remain unresolved at the end of each show, and the viewer must tune in the next day to find out what happens.

Sports programs deal with practically all sports in the United States. Many of these programs are broadcast in the evening or on weekends when parents—especially fathers—are most likely to be watching. Sports programs have one advantage over almost all other forms of TV programming—they contain "instant replay." That means a segment of the game can be presented again by the camera because the picture was kept on tape or film. You can see a part of the game a second or even a third time. This is especially useful when there is question about a foul in a game or a winning point.The camera in effect repeats the play for the audience. If this happened in a dramatic show or during a comedy, it would seem strange to us to see the action repeated. That would take away from the effect the writer had in mind—to make his story seem as natural as possible and as close to real life.

Talk shows such as "Oprah Winfrey" or "Donahue" are very popular on television. On these programs a host or hostess interviews famous people or experts in various fields who offer the viewers some new or unusual information. Often entertainers sing, dance, or enact a part from a current play or movie, and writers introduce and talk about their new books. Occasionally people such as drug addicts, single parents, adopted children, or handicapped persons will discuss and share their lives with the viewing public. Sometimes a person with an unusual experience appears on a talk show and describes it to the audience. This may be someone who has survived a disaster, seen a UFO, or made some important discovery in the sciences. A very high percentage of people interviewed on talk shows or even "news" shows are "celebrities" who are promoting a new film or rock concert. It may be important to help children to recognize that there are many people in fields other than popular entertainment or sports who make valuable contributions to our lives.

Variety shows are primarily for entertainment. Celebrity specials for example, feature comedians, singers, dancers, and musicians. We can see ridiculous scenes on variety shows or sometimes a clever comic will satirize serious issues and institutions, such as politics, religion, and the government. Variety shows usually have a host or hostess such as Johnny Carson who appears each time.

Finally, we have the **news programs.** Television news can instantly bring us in touch with every part of the world and create a personal feel in a news story. These programs are usually made up of three segments—international news, national news, and human interest stories. The newsperson usually presents the most important news story first and saves the lighter human interest stories (the rescue of a child from a burning building, an elderly person's special birthday, a reunion of a family after many years, etc.) for later. Too often in the last decade so-called morning news shows have become settings for interviewing entertainers promoting their upcoming appearance or films.

It is a difficult task for a news team to select the events for an evening news program. One half hour of the evening news may entail a full day of preparation, including the gathering of the news, writing, rewriting, editing, filming various segments, and making decisions about the order of presentation, the placement of commercials, and how long each segment of news should run.

TV news writers have the difficult job of presenting all the news and still leaving room for nightly features such as sports, weather, food tips, and movie and play reviews. Sometimes networks can present a subject in greater depth by using a

documentary format, a news program which reports at length on special subjects such as farmers, nuclear energy, forests, or endangered animals. Reporters can use interview techniques, library film, actual pictures of the event or of the subject, and a variety of camera techniques to keep the audience interested.

In addition to news programs and documentaries, we have the **television news magazine,** such as "Hard Copy," "48 Hours," "20/20" and "60 Minutes." We get some news, some in-depth coverage of a special topic, and some features involving interesting personalities. Sometimes there are in-depth interviews conducted with one or several people, such as "Meet the Press" or the "MacNeil-Lehrer News Hour." The people interviewed here usually offer their opinions about important events concerning politics, the economy, and international affairs. We also see **special coverage** news programs when an entire show is devoted to detailing some current news story, such as a disaster (like a flood or an earthquake), a visit from a dignitary (like the Pope), or a program highlighting the elections or a political debate.

Newspeople often try to present news stories that can be accompanied by interesting pictures. A news item about a flood, for example, is always more dramatic than an item about the cost of living, even though the latter information directly affects a far greater number of people. Choices must be made constantly about how to present the news, but most newspeople try to be fair and aim to be truthful.

Special Words and Ideas
for Children to Review

Adventure programs "MacGyver," "Quantum Leap," "Rescue 911"

Cartoons "Smurfs," "Yogi Bear," "Superfriends," "Los Niños"

Comedy programs "Alf," "Who's the Boss," "Growing Pains," "The Cosby Show"

Dramas "Young Riders," "Wonderworks"

Documentaries "60 Minutes," and "48 Hours" include brief documentaries

Educational programs "3–2–1 Contact," "The Electric Company," "Jacques Cousteau," "Reading Rainbow," "The Voyage of The Mimi"

Game shows "Wheel of Fortune," "Family Feud"

News programs "CBS Evening News," "The MacNeil-Lehrer Report," "NBC News"

Serials "All My Children," "As the World Turns," "Another World"

Sports programs "NFL Football," "World Series," "Wide World of Sports"

Talk shows "Sally Jessie Raphael," "Phil Donahue," "Oprah Winfrey"

Variety shows Johnny Carson's "Tonight Show," "Black Showcase," "Bob Hope Specials," "Carol Burnett Specials"

Discussion Ideas

Use the list of types of programs as your starting point. Talk about sample programs for each type. Try to get your children to point out the special characteristics of each category, and why a particular program falls into it.

Find out if your children prefer one type of program format compared to another. Ask them why.

Watch a type of program that your children rarely watch. See, for example, if you can interest them in documentaries or educational programs.

Discover which kinds of programs the family generally prefers to view together. Have the children list these and talk about why these particular programs appeal to the family. What are the elements in the program?

Older children need to be encouraged to read newspapers if they want a more detailed account of an event. By the time children are in junior high school, they may be cynical about television. It is therefore important for them to understand that TV content is controlled to some extent. Children in the middle grades (5 to 8) are old enough to learn how TV news can at times appear to distort an event by presenting only part of the story. For example, you and your children may want to discuss how a political speech may be shown on TV. The director may choose to show the part of the speech where an audience cheered enthusiastically, or where they heckled the speaker. Very often, there will not be time to show both parts.

In a case like this the complete story is not being presented, and a viewer may be left with an inaccurate impression of what actually took place. Even if the newscaster describes the "other side," most viewers will remember what they *saw* more vividly than what they *heard.*

Suggested Readings:

What Parents Should Know about TV
Channing L. Bete Co.Inc.
200 State Road
South Deerfield, MA 01373

The Question of TV Viewing and Children
 New Jersey Coalition for Better TV Viewing
P.O. Box 2381
Trenton, NJ 08607

Activity 1

Explain the program categories to your child. When you watch television with your child, see if he can tell you the correct categories for the programs. Here is a sample of an activity you can do together.

TV Program Categories

Name one or two programs that belong under the categories listed.

Cartoon   Comedy

_____   _____

Drama   Game Show

_____   _____

Movie   News

_____   _____

Sports   Talk show

_____   _____

Serial (soap opera): a continuing story

_____

Documentary: a program about a real event

_____

Kindergarten and first grade children may just name the type of program rather than write it. They may only be able to describe a few of the programs, such as sports, cartoons, comedies, or game shows. Try not to expect too much from your child, and don't frustrate your child by demanding that she learn more than she is ready to learn.

Activity 2

Ask older children (grades 5 to 8) to write down a typical day's viewing by listing how many of each type of program they watched. For example, on Monday a child might watch one news program, one variety program, and three comedy shows. If your child wants to, he can keep a record for a week, and fill in each category.

Activity 3

Different Types of TV Programs

Be a TV Detective. Try to find pictures of each type of TV program. Look in the newspaper or in *TV Guide* for pictures that match the shows below.

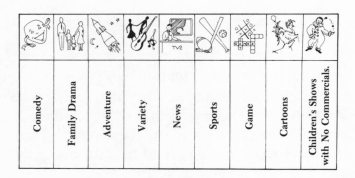

Comedy	Family Drama	Adventure	Variety	News	Sports	Game	Cartoons	Children's Shows with No Commercials.

Activity 4

1. Watch the news with your child. Write down the order of presentation. On another night, turn to a different channel. Watch the news. Was the order the same—did international news come first, for example?

2. Compare a news story in your evening newspaper with a story on TV. What items are omitted?

3. Are different kinds of products advertised during network news than on local news? Why?

instructs the camera operators over the telephone *headset*. While the engineers are getting their equipment ready, the cast members are busy putting on their costumes and makeup. (All actors have to wear makeup; without it, the bright studio light would make them look pale.)

Show your child the names of people who do this kind of work, before and after a favorite program. Explain that the lists of names are called *credits,* because they give credit to the people who helped.

Special Words and Ideas for Children to Review

Actor   a man or woman who plays a certain character in a TV program

Airwaves   carry electrical signals from the TV studio to your TV set at home

Antenna   The air is full of TV signals sent from many stations. These signals are caught by an antenna.

Audio   the sound part of a program

Broadcast   to send pictures and sound by television

Cable TV   a method of transmitting TV pictures into your home through wires, just the way the telephone wires bring in messages.

Camera operator   the person who works the TV cameras. The camera operator takes orders from the director.

Credits   the list of names of the people who make a TV program

Director   the person in charge of making the TV program. The director decides which props to use, how the actors should act, and which camera to use at a certain time.

Engineer the person who is in charge of the electrical equipment at a TV station, such as the TV lights, video and audio equipment, and the TV cameras

Microphone also called mike. Microphones pick up the voices and sounds that are part of a television program. The sound is changed, like the picture, into electrical signals.

Network a group of TV stations connected by electrical signals all over the country so that they can all receive the same TV programs and commercials. The three largest commercial networks are ABC, CBS, and NBC. Since TV programs cost a lot of money to make, TV stations can't make many programs. The networks make TV programs that are shown all over the United States, so they are able to sell broadcast time to sponsors at a higher rate than local TV stations.

Picture what you see on your TV

Producer the person who creates and organizes TV programs. The producer is in charge of finding and spending the money it takes to make a TV program. He or she makes other important decisions, such as which script or actors to use.

Rehearse to practice using the words and actions used in the program

Satellite signals are relayed instantly to a responder in orbit about the earth (a device which receives and re-transmits signals) which enables a program to be received in this country by anyone with a special, giant dish-like receiver situated near the building. TV signals can also be relayed over oceans.

Scene TV programs are divided into different parts. Each part is called a scene.

Script the written text of both the picture and sound parts of a TV program

Script writer the person who writes the story to be used in a TV program

Sound what you hear on your TV

Studio a special room for making television productions. Each studio is soundproof. Most studios have at least two TV cameras and special kinds of lights.

TelePrompTer while television news reporters or interviewers on talk shows seem to be talking naturally or addressing the audience spontaneously they are almost always reading what they say from a screen off-camera that displays the words they should say or the questions they should ask. This is the TelePrompTer.

Television set a receiver that picks up electric signals in the air and turns them into the picture and sound on your TV screen

TV camera A picture begins in the TV camera. There is no film in it. Its job is to change the picture it sees into an electrical signal that can be sent through wires and across space. Three or four large studio cameras are used to take pictures on an average TV program.

TV screen the front of the TV set where you see the picture

TV station where the TV studios, cameras, and other TV equipment are located. The electrical signals that are carried through the airwaves to your TV set at home come from the TV station. Nowadays most shows except some of the news is taped beforehand so all the station does is play tapes.

Video the picture part of the program

Videotape   The sound and picture electrical signals are recorded on videotape so that a TV program can be edited
and broadcast at a later time. Videotape can be played
back immediately.

Discussion Ideas

Show your child a photograph from a newspaper. Let your
child use a magnifying glass to discover the black and white
dots of which it is composed. A comic strip can be examined
to see how color dots are used. The following questions may
be helpful.

1. What colors are the dots?

2. What colors do you see when you look at the picture
   from farther away?

3. Why do you see shades of gray in a picture made up of
   black and white dots?

4. Why do you see colors that aren't really there?

Help you child see that the TV picture is also made up of dots
or grids.

Using the diagram of the transmission process, go over the
process with your child.

Briefly explain the different jobs involved in making a TV
program. After you have explained this information, watch a
program with your child.

TV Magic: Effects and Special Effects

When Superman bends a steel girder with his hand, when Spiderman leaps from a tall building and lands unharmed on the ground, or when Sam on "Quantum Leap" goes back in time, a kind of "magic" is taking place before our eyes. Adults recognize in a general way that the camera and special-effects team is at work, but children may need help in understanding how reality is distorted on television. Many different effects and special effects are used to make television programs appear more interesting and exciting. These techniques sometimes help children to understand a program's plot, but they can also be distracting and confusing, especially for younger children who have trouble distinguishing between reality and fantasy.

The purpose of this chapter is to help children learn more about the effects and special effects used on television, including camera shots, slow motion, sound effects, different kinds of props, and editing. If children can understand how and why these techniques are used, they can learn more from the programs they watch.

What You Need to Know

All television programs use effects and special effects. Close-up shots on news programs, for example, focus one's attention on what the newscaster is saying. Or when a photograph accompanies a story, the camera backs away from the newscaster for a long shot so one can look at the photograph *and* the newscaster.

Action programs, programs with superheroes or science fiction characters, and many other shows that are popular with children use a greater assortment of special effects, which children can learn to recognize. Although these techniques affect children greatly, they have been studied more often by advertisers than educators. Advertisers have learned, for example, that children will keep their eyes on commercials that use exciting special effects and that quickly change from one camera shot to another. "Sesame Street," "The Electric Company," "3–2–1 Contact" and other educational television programs have imitated the quick pace of commercials to keep young children watching the set. However, these techniques are not necessarily useful in helping children *understand* what they are watching.

Research conducted by Gavriel Salomon at Hebrew University in Israel and by John Wright and Aletha Huston and their colleagues at the University of Kansas has shown that certain camera effects help children understand programs. For example, when the camera zooms in for a close-up shot of an object in a room, and then zooms out again for a view of the whole room, a child can better understand exactly where the object is. This is important if the viewer is supposed to notice that the object is missing later in the program. However, if zoom shots or other effects are used to emphasize unimportant parts of a story, they will often distract and confuse young children. As a result young viewers may forget the more important elements of the story. If, for example, a child watches an action program with many exciting violent scenes, he or she may forget the line of the plot or fail to realize that the "bad guys" are punished in the end. Researcher Mary Field and her associates in England found that children between the ages of seven and eleven had difficulty with long shots, unexpected loud sounds, blaring music, and abrupt cutting from one scene to another.

We are also concerned about the impact special effects may have on children's imagination and creativity. When a child reads a fairy tale, he or she must imagine the scene and think about what is happening. But when a child watches the same fairy tale on TV, all the fantasy and creativity is in the hands of the producer, director, actors, camera operators, and program editors, The child can passively watch the program without ever thinking about the story. However, if your child understands how effects and special effects are used, any program can become a "puzzle" to think about and solve.

Changing reality through the use of a camera is known as a *camera effect.* The simplest way to do this is to move the camera. If, for example, the camera is moved from side to side, the viewer will see different parts of the room as if he were turning his head. This technique, *panning,* can show that different people in the televised room see it from different views, or panning can be used simply to take the viewer from one character to another. This kind of movement makes a program more interesting than if the camera merely showed the viewer the whole room for the entire scene.

It is also possible to change the way the camera sees just by changing its height. Placing the camera down low can make an actor look bigger, and placing the camera up high can make an actor look smaller.

Changing the Height of the Camera

  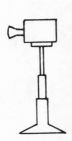

Here is a picture of Ralph taken with a TV camera.

When the TV camera is held near the ground and is TILTED
UP, this is how Ralph will look.

When the TV camera is held up high and is TILTED DOWN,
this is how Ralph will look.

Many television cameras have a zoom lens that can zoom into the picture for a close-up view, then zoom out again. The lens can zoom very quickly or so slowly that you hardly notice it. You can probably find an example of these basic camera shots on any television program.

THE ZOOM LENS:
ZOOMING IN AND ZOOMING OUT

Here is a picture of Tommy taken by a TV camera.

This TV camera has a special lens called a ZOOM lens. Without moving the TV camera, you can very quickly make things look closer or farther away by turning the ZOOM lens. When you turn the ZOOM lens very quickly to make things look closer, you are ZOOMING IN. This is how Tommy would look if the TV camera ZOOMED IN.

  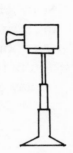

When you turn the ZOOM lens on the TV camera very quickly to make things look farther away from you, you are ZOOMING OUT. This is how Tommy would look if the TV camera ZOOMED OUT.

When the director of the "Sesame Street" program wants to show us a close-up of a letter or a number he uses the camera effect of a *zoom* which makes the letter or number appear very large on the screen or he can zoom out and the letter or number can appear quite small. There are other effects as well, including lighting and sound effects such as rain, lightning, and thunder. One can create a lightning effect simply by moving a piece of cardboard in front of a studio light. Sounds of rain and thunder can be recorded and then played back whenever they are needed.

All the effects in television that take us from one picture to another require the use of a *switcher*. The director can use this device to *cut* quickly from one shot to another; he can *dissolve* slowly to the next picture; and he can have one scene slowly *fade* away as the next scene fades in. The switcher also enables the director to *wipe* from one shot to the next. A wipe, as illustrated on the next page, can move in many different directors and assume a variety of shapes.

Wipes

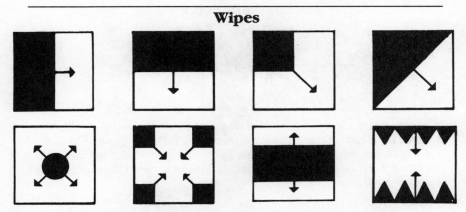

Top row: horizontal wipe, vertical wipe, corner wipe,
diagonal wipe; bottom row: circle wipe, four-corner wipe,
horizontal-split wipe, horizontal sawtooth wipe.

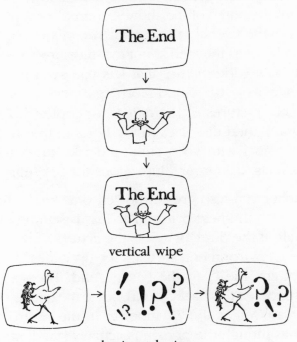

vertical wipe

horizontal wipe

The Split Screen

You can create a split screen effect by stopping a wipe in the middle of the screen. Each half of the screen will present a different picture. To set up for a split screen one camera must put one object in the left half of the viewfinder, the other in the right half. The unnecessary part of each picture is then wiped out.

The switcher also lets the director superimpose words and pictures on a main picture. The "Today" show, for example, opens with the name of the show "supered" on a picture, then dissolves to the hosts in the studio. The picture cuts to close-ups of the hosts as they tell about that morning's program, and then cuts to a wide picture that lets you see the newscaster. On another network, "Good Morning America" uses wipes to put together pictures of the different people who appear on the program, then dissolves to the hosts in the studio. Watch these programs with your child and take turns naming the camera effects, using our illustrations for references.

The switcher can also create the "chroma-key" effect. In the illustration on the next page, an actress is standing in front of a blue wall. If the director wants the actress to be standing in a different environment, he can set up slides or a moving picture of any locale in the background. The actress in the studio cannot see this background, but to the television viewers at home (as well as the TV monitor in the control room), it will look as though the person is actually standing in front of the scene. In the picture it seems as if the actress is standing in an actual forest; in fact she is *still* standing in front of the blue wall. This technique is called *chroma-key* and is used often on television. News programs, for example, always use chroma-key to show photographs behind newscasters. Sports programs also use this technique frequently. When sportscasters introduce a football game with an entire stadium in the background, they are really sitting in front of a blue wall in the studio with a shot of the stadium chroma-keyed behind them.

Chroma-Key

(left) Color slide of trees provides background for the key effect.

(center) Studio camera takes a picture of a woman standing in front of an evenly lighted blue background.

(right) The completed chroma key effect transports the woman into the landscape.

When directors want people to disappear on TV, or when they want other impossible events to occur, they can choose from a variety of special effects. Programs using fantasy often show people vanishing instantly. Creating this illusion is a relatively simple matter. In the photograph on the next page, the magician waves the magic wand and holds very still while the little boy simply walks away. The director won't want the TV audience to see the boy leaving, so he simply *edits* that part out. The finished scene will look as if the boy suddenly disappeared.

Editing: Making Someone Disappear

Editing can create other special effects as well. When you watch a superhero jumping higher than humanly possible, you may notice that the jump doesn't happen in one picture. Instead, there are usually three views of the actor jumping. In the first view the actor has started to jump. In the second view he seems to be moving quickly through the air. That is really a second jump, which may have been from a trampoline. The third view shows the actor landing at the top. This is actually the end part of a third jump. The three taped jumps are then edited together to look like one long jump. Parts which show the trampoline, the end of the first jump, or the beginning of the third jump are edited out. Scenery can also be changed to make the jump seem even higher.

Editing: A Bionic Jump

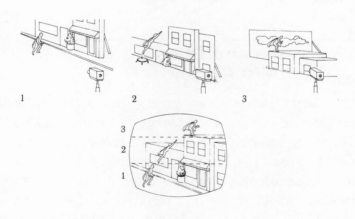

Another kind of special effect is *slow motion,* a technique often used on superhero programs to emphasize the action (notice how many fighting sequences are shown in slow motion). *Fast motion* is sometimes used on these same programs to make the hero's running seem superfast. Both effects are achieved simply by speeding up or slowing down the tape or camera.

There are many other kinds of special effects, and often several of them are used together. For example, if a program shows two people in a car chase, the actors are probably not in a real automobile, but in a machine that has car seats, a steering wheel, and no tires. The machine can't be driven, but it shakes as if it were swerving around corners. The camera tapes close-up shots of the actors' faces so the viewer does not see most of the machine. Meanwhile, a chroma-key of a videotape of streets and other cars is used as a background for the scene. Sound effects of screeching tires and honking horns are also used. The tape of the people talking is then edited together with the tape of a real car chase.

Special Words and Ideas for Children to Review

Chroma-key   This is a way of combining two entirely different pictures so that they appear to be one solid picture. The actor can be put right into a scene, not just in front of it. It is used to make actors look much larger or smaller than their surroundings; to make it look as if they are moving quickly from one place to another; or to make people who are actually in different places appear to be together.

Close-up   a camera shot which makes the object or person seem very close to you

Cut   a quick change from one camera to another, without an overlap of the pictures

Dissolve   a slow change from one camera shot to another, so that you see both shots for a short time

Edit   to electronically "cut out" unwanted parts of a videotape recording of a TV program and save the pieces that are wanted. The result looks like a single continuous program.

Freeze-frame   holding a single, nonmoving picture on the screen

Pan   turning the camera from side to side, so that you see what you would see if you were turning your head

Shot   each picture that the camera takes

Slow-motion   The normal speed of the camera is slowed down, making the action look slower than it is.

Split screen   The screen is divided into two or more parts and each camera shows its picture on one part of the screen.

Wipe   an electrical effect that makes one picture seem to push another picture off the TV screen. Wipes can be made in many shapes, including circles growing larger or a line moving across the screen.

Zoom   Without moving the TV camera, objects or people can be made to look closer or farther away by using a zoom lens attached to the camera. *Zoom-in* means turning the zoom lens to make an object look closer than it really is. *Zoom-out* means turning the zoom lens to make an object look father away than it really is.

Discussion Ideas

Can TV superheroes really do all those impossible things? If they can't, how is it that we see them do these things on TV? Special effects can make us think we're seeing something that isn't really happening. It's a bit like magic.

Go over the words and effects with your child. Find some programs that use these effects. Ask your child to name them as you view the program together. Keep a list of the effects you find. See how many you can discover in just one evening.

Special Reading

The following book would be helpful for this lesson: MacDonald Educational *The Movies,* a picture book explaining movies and cartoons.

Activities

1. Pick one of the following special effects. How do you do it?

   a. An eye sees a man a long distance away—the eye is large on the TV screen

   b. A person turns into a monster

   c. A witch makes a girl disappear

2. Which programs use slow motion? Why do they use slow motion? What would the scene look like without slow motion?

3. Write a story about a superhero. At the end of the story, list the kinds of special effects you might use if you made a TV program about your story.

4. Make three drawings to show how a superhero jump is made for a TV program.

5. Which TV programs show people disappearing? Make a list.

CHAPTER SEVEN

Real and Pretend on TV

In a discussion about creativity in writing fiction and in scientific research Albert Einstein once said, "When I examine myself and my methods of thought, I come to the conclusion that the gift of fantasy has meant more to me than my talent for absorbing positive knowledge." (*The New York Times Magazine,* February 18, 1979).

Imagination is a basic human characteristic, probably with us at birth, but which develops according to an individual's upbringing and education. Our imaginative capacities can help us reconstruct old memories and form new thoughts, and they can provide us with a medium for future planning, self-entertainment and aesthetic appreciation or creativity. In this chapter, we examine the very critical impact that television and make-believe play may have on a child's imagination.

There is reason to believe that daydreaming originates in the fantasy play of childhood. Evidence indicates, for example, that children fantasize as early as eighteen months to two years of age, and by three years of age one can observe a considerable amount of make-believe play. In a whole series of studies we have seen a variety of constructive possibilities for such pretend play in early child development.

The Value of Imagination for Children's Development

We list here some of the specific benefits for children between the ages of three and six who are able to engage in games of fantasy. We know of such advantages of early make-believe games because we can observe the differences between children who show such patterns early and those who don't. The fact is that by ages three or four some children are already regularly engaging in pretend play whenever they can.

Self-entertainment and Positive Emotionality

We find considerable evidence that kindergarten and pre-school children involved in make-believe play show positive emotions and smile and laugh often. Children who have this capacity to create an imaginary world appear happier than those who do not engage in games of fantasy.

Delaying Capacity, Waiting Behavior, and Development of Defenses

Freud pointed out that one function of the ego is to defer gratification and to delay rash, impulsive behavior. Our evidence clearly indicates that children who have the capacity for fantasizing are better able to tolerate periods of delay, to defer immediate gratification, resist temptation, and to develop stronger defenses against the expression of anger and distress.

Vocabulary and Cognitive Skills

Children often talk out loud when they engage in make-believe games. By doing so, they can hear their own words and try out new combinations of words and phrases. Our data show that children who play games of fantasy also have command of a more complex vocabulary and grammar.

Empathy

Research indicates that children who engage in make-believe games take different roles as part of these games. Sometimes they are the heroes, sometimes the "bad guys." They have periods of victory and moments of failure. As a result of such role-playing, children learn to empathize with the plight and emotions of others.

Role-Rehearsal

The very nature of make-believe play requires children to act out many of the roles they must adopt later in their lives. In kindergarten, children learn how to deal with these roles through the use of symbolic and imaginary games. Children actually rehearse games such as school, going to the doctor, taking a trip, etc. In effect they are preparing themselves for a wide variety of situations they will have to confront as they grow up. Naturally, in a more extended way this role-rehearsal forms a part of the adult's fantasy capacities—a person willing to play out many possible situations will be better prepared for those situations when they actually occur. There is even evidence which indicates that gymnasts, skiers, basketball players and other athletes who engage in mental as well as physical exercise do better than those who do not rely on their imagery and fantasy capacities as part of the training procedure.

Planning and Foresight

An important potential outgrowth of the skills in imagery and fantasy a child develops may be the capacity for planning. We know that extremely impulsive adults and adolescents show very little evidence of imagination and fantasy on psychological tests. Early practice in pretend play may therefore be important in helping the child develop a mental set in which different possibilities and plans can be tried out before one embarks on a hasty course of action.

Aesthetic Appreciation and Creativity

Finally, evidence suggests that the imaginative capacity, particularly in later childhood, adolescence, and adult life, is related to the ability to appreciate the art forms. We have learned to play out some of our previous experiences on a mental screen. We also can relive scenes from movies or books or ballets, and we can enjoy in memory the fine moments of a symphonic concert or intricate sequences of play in an athletic event. The human imagination therefore has an important role not only in the development of our basic capacity to learn and organize new information, but in the more general enrichment of our day-to-day life.

We must quickly add one point about imagination for those who are inclined to think that imagery and fantasy processes reflect immature, neurotic, or psychotic forms of thought. Research evidence suggests that many individuals who are emotionally disturbed have failed to develop control over their imaginative resources. Often their fantasies are repetitive and extremely limited in scope. In many cases individuals who have had emotional difficulties or who were engaged in antisocial behavior have not learned to use their own imagery and fantasy capacities well. There is also evidence from research with children and from observations with adults that individuals who have developed their imaginative capacities are better able to differentiate between their own thoughts and hallucinations; that is, they have learned a more precise distinction between reality and fantasy by having practiced and identified fantasy experiences over the years.

Factors in Early Childhood Conducive to Imaginative Development

We are only beginning to explore what early childhood experiences cause children to engage more regularly in make-believe games. We shall briefly summarize here some of the major results from research, literature, and clinical observation.

One could argue that the child, in order to develop the imaginative capacity more fully, needs what might be called novel material or interesting information to assimilate. The eminent psychologist Jean Piaget, in his analysis of early childhood development, argued that a child tries to repeat and integrate new material with his previously established ideas. In the course of such attempted assimilation, we see playful behavior and much of what we often regard as "cute." A child of four was observed by his mother lining up all of his toy soldiers on the kitchen floor. When asked what he was doing, he replied, "I'm getting them ready to rescue Daddy. You were talking on the telephone and said he couldn't come home for dinner because he was tied up at work!"

There is reason to believe that children who have little opportunity to communicate with adults (or who don't have a chance to overhear more complex vocabulary) may participate less in make-believe play. There is also evidence that children from lower socioeconomic backgrounds use a very limited vocabulary. Studies in many crowded inner-city or culturally disadvantaged homes suggest that parents often talk very little to their children except for giving quick commands like "Be quiet," "leave your sister alone," "time to eat." When children from such backgrounds are given a chance to play make-believe games, their vocabulary becomes more diversified and new words and grammatical constructions are practiced. In homes where parents have the time or inclination to tell children stories, to talk about the family history or about their own childhoods, we find that children develop more elaborate and interesting plots in their make-believe play. If given the opportunity to engage in such play, children can expand their use of language.

Evidence also suggests that the amount of privacy a child has for practicing make-believe games may be important. Similarly, there are indications that toys that do not clearly symbolize a person, but are somewhat more neutral, such as blocks, Legos, or clay, will lend themselves to a greater variety of play situation.

Probably the most important factor in the development of children's imaginative capacities is their relationship with parents, uncles and aunts, older siblings, etc. The great German poet Goethe wrote:

> From Father I have looks and build
> And the serious conduct of living.
> My Mother gave me gaiety
> And zest for fantasizing.
>
> (Xenien)

We know from an increasing body of research that adults who take the time to play with, tell stories to, and read to children play a crucial role in the development of their imagination. Research has also shown that adults who get children involved in a game or a story and then gradually step away to allow the child's own interest and motivation to take over are most likely to encourage spontaneous make-believe play.

We have tried to make a strong case for encouraging imagination in children and ultimately in adults. We believe the imagination is of great importance not only for the emotional pleasures it can bring but also because it is tremendously useful in handling information, in planning, and in creative activities.

Those of us who listened to radio shows before television became so widespread were able to conjure up mental pictures of Buck Rogers, Flash Gordon, Jack Armstrong, and The Shadow. If we were to describe the characters or settings, we all would have different versions of their features, clothing, habits, and surroundings. We play a more active role listening to radio than we do while watching TV. Actually, research by psychologist Patricia Greenfield and her colleagues demonstrated that children provide more imaginative endings to an audio ("radio") story than to the same story presented audiovisually ("TV"). The authors suggest that the radio stories stimulate the children's imagination leading to the use of more imaginative words, events, and characters than TV. Television does not necessarily preclude the use of segments on a program from being copied by children. We know from our own research experiences that many nursery school children imitate sequences from television programs viewed in the past. One vivid scene we noted was a child pretending she was Wendy. She sat in a makeshift house "cooking," while her friend pretended she was flying, spreading her arms like wings, running around the room shouting "I'm Peter Pan." Two others were acting out the pirate scene replete with make-believe alligators and a cruel Captain Hook.

It seems likely that the highly imaginative child needs to withdraw from the set periodically to actively play out the material he sees. Constant stimulus of television programming may interfere with the child's own "game plans." Some children watch television with intense concentration and thus do not withdraw from the set to play out material. We need to compare these two viewing styles to see whether or not the highly imaginative child views television with the same degree of intensity as the less imaginative child. Perhaps intensive viewing has no effect on a child's ability to *extract from television,* and the capacity for imagination is more critical than the degree of concentration. We have found, for example, that during a viewing of "Mister Rogers' Neighborhood" most of the children in our study did *not* stay glued to the television screen. Yet when compared to children who were riveted to a showing of "Sesame Street," the children viewing "Mister Rogers' Neighborhood" did as well in tests pertaining to material remembered from the show as did those watching "Sesame Street." It may be that Fred Rogers' repetition of various words and phrases enabled the children to process the material even though the set did not hold their undivided attention.

We are interested in whether or not television can lead to imitation of events which are later brought into a child's make-believe game. Although little research has focused on television's impact on the imaginative potential of children, numerous studies have dealt with the positive effects of television. The question of extending behaviors such as cooperation, sharing, and helping (what psychologists call prosocial behaviors) to instances other than direct imitation of acts portrayed on the television programs has been demonstrated. Such interactions as altruism and sympathy are portrayed in television programs and in commercials. There is now evidence that children can become more caring after exposure to programs that deal with positive values such as "Degrassi High" and "Freestyle" for older children and "Sesame Street" and "Mr. Rogers' Neighborhood" for preschoolers.

What Research Tells us about Reality and Fantasy

There are advantages for the use of video for teaching social skills. For example, video activates multiple senses—vision, hearing. Combined with discussion, ideas on a program can be reinforced; role-models acting in positive ways enable a child to identify with a well-liked character; and if a video tape is used, particular segments can be played repeatedly to reinforce an idea.

In one of our studies, we compared the effects of two kinds of children's programs on the imagination of preschoolers. We found that children who were rated low in imagination at the beginning of the experiment and were exposed to ten sessions of the "Mister Rogers' " program over a two-week period made significant gains in imagination when compared to children who viewed "Sesame Street" for that same period. The "Mister Rogers' " program, with its clear-cut distinction between reality and a make-believe kingdom, appears to stimulate imagination, as well as socially useful behaviors in children. Psychologists Lynette Friedrich and Aletha Stein also found gains in three- to five-year-old children's imagination after exposure to the "Mister Rogers' " program. The experimental condition involving prosocial television, related play materials, and teacher training and involvement produced the most consistent effects on both positive social interaction with peers and imaginative play.

In one long-term project we were studying imagination and its relationship to television. We observed 340 children to collect data on their imagination, aggression, concentration, cooperation, peer interaction, and mood states. We interviewed the children about television viewing habits and TV-related games and toys they owned, and we also questioned them about imaginary playmates, favorite games, whether or not they had "pictures in their head," and if they had day-dreams. The parents had been keeping detailed records of what programs the children viewed during two-week probes every three months. Parents were also interviewed about their children's viewing habits, and whether their children had imaginary playmates. Data suggest that children who were light television viewers reported significantly more imaginary playmates than those who were heavy television viewers. It is interesting to note that girls were more likely to use both female and male TV characters as imaginary playmates (Superman, Wonder Woman), while boys only identified with male superheroes. The children who had imaginary playmates also exhibited more adaptive play and more developed language, in addition to watching less television than the other subjects.

Psychologist Robert P. Snow asked 50 preadolescent children what their favorite programs were, and if they thought the shows were "real" or "make-believe." All of the children could identify cartoons as make-believe and news as real (although there was a split of opinion about family situation comedies), and they were able to recognize a difference between their own make-believe play and real situations. The children also stated a preference for make-believe television which they could relate to their own play. Interestingly, these children did not describe "Road Runner," a cartoon, as violent, because they classified it as make-believe. Thus, when the child can distinguish between real and make-believe, the impact of violent action in fantasy shows is lessened, according to Snow. Furthermore, in this study the children were also able to make distinctions between "funny" and "serious" violence in television.

In contrast to Snow's subjects, who were all in the ten-to-twelve age range, psychologist Ralph J. Garry studied preschool and primary-grade children. Garry found that these younger children accepted what they saw on television as real. Westerns were less disturbing to them than crime and detective stories, which were closer to real life. A great deal depends on how similar a situation on TV is to one that a child observes in his or her own life. According to Garry, events on television which portray children in important roles have a greater impact on young viewers, especially if they are of the same age and sex.

Grant Noble, at the University of New England in Australia, has carried out numerous studies examining effects of television on children. He found that children played less constructively after viewing realistic aggression, and more constructively after seeing very artificial or ritualized aggression—e.g., knights jousting or cowboy shoot-outs. Noble also suggested that five-year-olds have more difficulty in determining what is real than do six-, seven-, and eight-year-olds. He found that in retelling stories they had seen, the five-year-olds added people and objects that were not in the film. They were also unable to comprehend when a story ended. They embellished stories with their own imaginative people and ideas. Research by John Murray and Kathy Krendl of Kansas State University supports Noble's results. They found that fifth graders who watched an average of 25.5 hours per week were more likely to believe that characters and actions on television programs were real compared to lighter viewers who disavowed the reality of television.

Psychologists Elihu Katz and David Foulkes reported that middle-class children experiencing difficult parent-child relations and children isolated from their peers were heavier television viewers, with the latter group specifically preferring adventure stories. This use of fantasy-oriented media appeared to be related to disparities between a child's aspirations and those of his peers or parents. The authors wondered whether such programming drained off discontent and enabled children to understand themselves better, or if it led a child to withdraw from the real world and to confuse real situations with fantasy. Another study dealing with children's fantasy life and its relationship to television found that children who were heavy viewers of television reported more anxious, hostile and generally unpleasant fantasies on a measure of imagery.

In some of our own research, children in grades 3, 4, and 5 who watched fantasy-violent programs were less cooperative, less successful in their interpersonal relationships, less happy and less imaginative. We also found that children who spent more time reading watched fewer fantasy-violent programs. They may have been able to satisfy their interest in adventure through reading and imagination, and relied less on television as a source of excitement.

In a study of 30 children in Australia exposed to either "This Is Your Life" or "Sports Day," Grant Noble reported that 14 thought that the people on the set had spoken directly to them, and 6 of the children answered back. The reality of the set for these children involved them in "conversation" with the television characters. In our work with preschoolers we have heard them respond to Mister Rogers when he asked questions. Actually, Fred Rogers allows this response by use of "still" moments, when he does not talk, but expects a child to interact with him. This gives a child the opportunity to repeat the message and store it.

Modeling behavior is important and, as mentioned, has powerful effects on children. One area that remains relatively untapped is the use of television in day-care centers as a model to teach children how to play and become more imaginative. If teachers had materials related to specific television formats, they could serve as mediators and reinforce particular messages, ideas, or concepts through related activities. In one of our studies, for example, when Mister Rogers presented a puppet show about "Jack and the Beanstalk," a nursery school teacher then very successfully used materials and puppets to get the children to use their imaginations.

Our experience leads us to believe that if children learn how to play and use their imaginations actively, they can make a clearer distinction between reality and fantasy. The child who says "let's pretend" has had the practice of moving between the real world and the one of his imagination. If television presents material confusing to the young child, parents can help clarify these confusions by watching programs with their children and explaining how certain effects introduce the world of fantasy on television.

What You Need to Know

Television employs many techniques to create illusions and a sense of fantasy. People seem to talk to each other freely, without pausing or hemming and hawing the way we do in real-life conversations. They snap clever remarks and "put downs" back and forth at each other with a speed we can never attain when we're conversing with people. This illusion of rapid speech, of quickness of wit, is produced by careful re-hearsals, and by editing out of a tape the natural pace of speech. Thus, even many of the "live" events on TV are prerecorded on tape and carefully edited. Sometimes the "voice-over" comments of sportscasters, which show great perception about a particular play or athletic maneuver, are actually recorded *after* the events by simply having the speaker's remarks recorded as he watches a video playback. To the viewer it looks as if the sportscaster knows more than he does.

Editing and "smoothing out" a tape of real people on talk shows or news programs is one way of creating an *illusion* of reality. Another way of creating a sense of reality can be seen in "docudramas," films based on real events but with actors portraying the actual persons whose lives are depicted. Explain to your child that these TV dramas all use professional actors to play persons who once lived.

TV also presents actors who portray characters that seem very real although actually they are fictional productions of the screen writers. Mike on "Growing Pains," for example, seems to many people as real as someone they know from school, and Roseanne Barr plays the fictional character Roseanne so convincingly that many people confuse the actress and the character.

There are also programs like "Quantum Leap" or "Highway to Heaven" which depict actors doing things that we know are impossible. Cartoons portray characters performing impossible deeds as well; although children understand that the people they see in these programs are not real.

It may be easy for children to understand that drawings are not real, but it is not so easy for them to understand when actors create illusions. Children may believe, for example, that actors are hitting each other in fights when in fact they are missing one another entirely. By using a variety of techniques, such as furniture which breaks easily; sound effects, and menacing music, a TV director can very effectively create the illusion that characters in fights are being hurt.

Many other methods can be employed to distort reality: make-up can be used to help characters look strange; the camera can make people look small like the Lilliputians on "Gulliver's Travels," or enormous like the beast on "Beauty and the Beast;" costumes can add to the fantasy or make-believe element in programs; and lighting effects can create the illusion of bright sunshine or darkness.

Special Words and Ideas
for Children to Review

Cartoons or animation   Separate drawings are photographed one at a time on film or videotape. When they are all shown together, it looks like the cartoon characters are moving.

Costumes   clothes and jewelry worn by the actors to make them look like the characters that they pretend to be

Fiction   a pretend or made-up story

Live   a TV program that is broadcast at the same time it is really happening

Makeup   powder, lipstick, eyeshadow, and other cosmetics used on the skin to change an actor's appearance

Nonfiction   a story about something that has really happened

Props   furniture and other objects used by actors to make the set look like a real place

Stunts   difficult, dangerous, or unusual actions such as jumping through a window, falling out of a tall building, or driving a car at high speeds through city traffic

Taped   a TV program that is recorded on videotape so that mistakes can be taken out. The program is broadcast at a later time.

Discussion Ideas

1. If your child watches fantasy programs like "Highway to Heaven," "Quantum Leap," "Alf" or "Superboy" ask your child: "Is Superboy a real person? Do the people on that program really exist? How do you know? How can you tell when something on TV is real?"

2. Have your children name some programs that depict real people talking about real events; programs that have actors portraying real events; and programs with actors portraying realistic fictional events: "How can you tell the difference? What are actors? What is the difference between an actor and a character?" Include information about how makeup, costumes, and props make people or events seem different than they really are (e.g., "The Kennedys of Massachusetts").

3. Discussion of programs where animated characters portray realistic events: "In what ways are the Flintstones realistic?" (e.g., They do things most people do.) "In what ways are they pretend?" (e.g., Cave dwellers did not have dinosaurs for pets, did not drive cars, etc.)

4. Discussion of programs where animated characters portray impossible events: "In what ways are the Superfriends (animated Batman, Wonder Woman, etc.) realistic? In what ways are they pretend? What other animated characters do impossible things?"

5. Ask your child: "How are cartoon animals realistic? In what ways are most cartoon animals unrealistic? (Why are they portrayed as wearing clothes and living like

humans?) Name some animals that seem to survive impossible danger." (e.g., Road Runner and Wile E. Coyote fall off cliffs, but are never hurt for more than a few seconds.)

6. Have your child name some programs where actors engage in impossible actions. (Examples include "Star Trek," "Alien Nation," "Batman.") "How can you tell that these are not realistic?"

Suggested Readings

Children may want to read books that deal with real events that have also been depicted on TV programs. Your local library probably has children's books on the following:

Pearl Harbor   Helen Keller
Amelia Earhart   Harriet Tubman
Eleanor Roosevelt   Franklin Roosevelt
Martin Luther King   John F. Kennedy

ACTIVITY PAGE

Activities

1. Set up a chart like the one below. Your child can draw pictures or cut and paste pictures of a fantasy character, a real person, and a realistic character in the space provided. Then he or she can list the real people and television characters in the correct columns.

2. Have your child list the programs that he watched this week that had real people talking abut real events; then the programs that had animated characters. Which type of program did he watch more often?

Reality and Fantasy on TV

Look at the names listed at the bottom of this page. Have you seen any of these people on TV? Some of them are *fantasy characters,* some are *realistic characters,* and the rest are *real people.* Write the names of the characters or people that you have seen in the correct rows.

Fantasy Characters	Real People	Realistic Characters
_____	_____	_____
_____	_____	_____
_____	_____	_____

Alf	Sister Kate	Bill Cosby
Donald Duck	Roseanne Barr	Nichole (My Two Dads)
MacGyver	Teddy Z	Arvid (Head of the Class)
Pee Wee Herman	Fred Rogers	Mr. Spock
Popeye	Michael Fox	

Draw a TV Fantasy Character Here:	Draw a Real Person on TV Here:	Draw a Realistic TV Character Here:

3. Write a story or poem about an imaginary person.

4. Write a story about the things you did today. Would that make an interesting TV program? Now change the story to make it more exciting or funny.

5. List some characters that are portrayed by actors and as animated characters. Would you rather see cartoon characters, or would you rather watch a program where the same characters are portrayed by actors?

6. Draw a cartoon character.

7. Look in a TV guide to see if there are any documentaries or docudramas on TV this week. List them.

8. Which programs use music to create a feeling of mystery or suspense? List them. Watch carefully this week and write down the programs that use music. Turn off the music during an exciting part. How did you like it without music?

9. Make up a tune to go along with a television scene.

10. If you watch a program that shows a fighting scene, write down the sound effects, props, or makeup which made the scene seem real.

11. Draw a person. Draw the same person on another sheet of paper, then change his or her appearance as if you were using makeup (do not erase).

12. If you have watched a TV program about real people (Examples: "The Kennedys of Massachusetts," "A Woman Called Moses"), read a book about the same person.

How was the TV story different from the book?

Characters We Love and Hate: Learning about Ourselves through People We Meet on TV

Parents are a child's first model for developing a sense of identity. The young child regards his parents as powerful, perfect, beautiful. He is also aware of the seeming injustices a parent may bestow on him when he is punished or prevented from doing something he desires. This process of identification and search for self begins in early childhood, continues through adolescence, and, as some psychologists believe, goes on throughout one's life. Erik Erikson, a prominent psychologist, suggests that most children go through two stages of identification: One when they are about four to six years old, and another during adolescence. Identifying with parents of the same sex and learning the appropriate behavior for males and females in society is a task of childhood. During adolescence, young people must not only reaffirm their sexual identities, but begin to form mature sexual relationships and think about questions relating to ideologies, ethics, and occupational choices. With the advent of the women's movement, and the increasing changes in society concerning women's role, it is interesting to note that television still perpetuates many stereotyped sex-role models and lags behind the current trend toward expanded role models, especially for women.

As we will see in our lesson on stereotypes, television depicts males in a wider range of occupations than females. More males are in dramatic network programs, and in general both males and females are shown in stereotypic roles. We may therefore wonder whether or not these characters exert any influence over children's identification patterns.

As children get older and enter school, teachers become increasingly important in their lives, and even parents of other children offer them new models for identification. Television, movies, books, and magazines suggest different occupational models for children, and certainly the heroes and heroines in any story offer a young person physical and psychological models beyond the immediate family. In order to finally achieve a sense of self, a child must be aware of his own physical makeup, his strong points as well as his inadequacies; and he must develop a feeling of consistency in life-style which would include his own particular way of growing, thinking, dressing, acting, and achieving.

How, then, does television play a role in helping a child develop a sense of identity? Think of how many women imitate Vanna White's hairdo or clothing styles after seeing her as the hostess on "Wheel of Fortune." Ask yourself if you have ever bought a product because you believed it would help you look like a television superstar. TV characters and celebrities influence our choice of clothes, the way we talk, our hobbies and interests, the way we decorate our homes, and even the way we behave. Children are especially likely to imitate the clothes, hair styles, and behaviors of the TV characters that they admire. This may include using expressions from their favorite TV programs or pretending to be a favorite superhero.

Children usually find it easy to talk with each other about which television characters they like and dislike. However, they may have more difficulty expressing *why* they feel the way they do. This lesson provides parents with an excellent opportunity to learn more about their children's feelings, to help their children understand their own feelings, and for parents and children to discuss their values together.

What You Need to Know

You should first remind your child (as we've mentioned earlier) that most actors pretend to be different characters on television. You can use the example of Michael J. Fox who played Alex on "Family Ties." Your child may have also seen Michael J. Fox in movies such as "Back to the Future." Remind him that producers, directors, writers, and actors create these characters.

The next step is to help your child think about why people like certain TV characters. You may want to point out that we often like characters who are somewhat like us or who enjoy what we enjoy. Popular TV characters are often funny (like Alf, Dr. Huxtable or Roseanne) or strong and successful (like MacGyver).

Have you ever thought about why your child likes superheroes? Because children are relatively small and weak, with very little control over their environment, they enjoy watching characters who are powerful. They can vicariously enjoy the control that these characters have over other people. (Of course, adults often like these characters for the same reasons.) In one of our studies we found that the most consistent play theme over a year's time by both boys and girls involved characters from television—generally superheroes such as Batman and Wonder Woman. We also found that both boys and girls had imaginary playmates based on television characters, again superheroes.

One interesting result we noted in our research was that girls could identify with both male and female characters, but the boys seemed to prefer only the males. Children also enjoy and identify with television personalities who are warm, funny, silly, and daring. These characters can exert a considerable influence over a child. For example, years ago when Evel Knievel made his daring jumps on television, many children (especially boys) ended up in accidents using makeshift ramps and their bicycles. Even more ordinary TV characters, such as Alex on "Family Ties" or Nicole on "My Two Dads," can affect the behavior of a child.

In prime-time television there are more children, adolescents, and elderly people cast in situation comedies or dramas than in action-adventure programs. Action-adventure shows tend to feature young and middle-aged adults, and these are the programs favored by boys. In situation comedies children are often presented as "cute" or "good" and generally in limited roles while the adult characters are more central to the plots.

Results from a number of studies report that adolescents who spend more time watching television are more likely to reflect traditional sex-role stereotypes. Since children in early adolescence (ages 9–13 years old) watch more television than any other age group except the elderly, television's influence on beliefs and attitudes about gender and occupational roles is important, but must also be considered along with other sources of input in a child's experience. Research by Roberta Wroblewski and Aletha Huston at the University of Kansas suggests that boys show evidence that heavy watching of television is associated with more polarized occupational aspirations. Boys were more biased when they saw girls in traditional male jobs but girls were positive about female participation in masculine occupations on television.

Parents should also understand how children learn and respond to role models. According to researchers Craig Edelbrock and Alan Sugawara, female preschoolers have clearer expectations for adult feminine behavior than males have for male adult behavior. The researchers found that boys were more likely to prefer programs portraying males in play (not adult) activities. The researchers explain that children are first exposed in life to female adults (mothers, day-care workers, preschool teachers) and thus girls have clearer feminine adult role models to emulate. Boys, on the other hand, must eventually shift away from female to male role models. Because fathers may not be around as much, peers may serve as stronger models than adult male figures. Boys may also turn to TV, where indeed there are more men than women portrayed in exciting and interesting roles.

In addition to serving as role models, characters on detective programs and even on situation comedies may provide children with an outlet for their anger and frustrations. For example, children may identify with characters who express anger openly. They can do this by copying their style of walking, talking, and even their aggressive behaviors. If the characters are presented as powerful and competent, and receive rewards for their behavior, children may indeed try to emulate them.

You may want to help your child compare the negative and positive traits of television characters. Many young children (grades kindergarten through 4) do not understand what "personality traits" are. They may find it easier to talk about what characters do rather than what kind of people they are. The traits that they can talk about are relatively superficial: strength, attractiveness, popularity, and humor. Parents may want to encourage children in this age group to think of other traits as well, such as empathy, kindness, and helpfulness. Children in the middle grades (5 through 8) may also focus on a character's superficial traits at first, but they can easily be encouraged to make more sophisticated judgments. Parents may want to encourage these older children to talk about more subtle, positive traits such as altruism, affection, industriousness, and loyalty; and negative traits such as greed, vengefulness, and shallowness.

Work by psychologists Aletha Huston and Lynette Freidrich as well as our own research has indicated that positive role models on programs such as "Mister Rogers' Neighborhood" (for young children), "Black Beauty," and "Swiss Family Robinson" can improve cooperation, sharing, and turn-taking. Roderic Gorney, David Loye, and Gary Steele in California found a significant decrease in aggressive moods in adult males after just one week's exposure to TV programs which emphasize positive traits.

Encourage your child to think about the way characters behave in different situations. Children often like the predictability of characters; they enjoy knowing how a favorite TV character will act in any given situation. For this reason, children may enjoy watching a weekly program because they feel they know the characters personally.

As a parent you should be aware of your child's favorite characters. Have you ever heard your child discuss TV characters with friends? Friends' opinions often influence children's attitudes. And, of course, the script writers, directors, and actors also manipulate the audience's feelings about TV characters. For example, viewers know how they should feel about Jesse because they see how much other characters on "Full House" admire him. Children may like a TV character who is funny, but you can point out that the character has other admirable traits. And when children see detective characters on TV, these characters may appear admirable even though they sometimes kill people. You should make sure that your child understands that these characters are not admirable *because* they kill people. With these and other TV characters, children should understand that characters can be both good and bad.

By talking about television characters, children can learn about other people and themselves. Parents can help children understand why they like characters and how these feelings influence their own needs and goals.

Special Words and Ideas for Children to Review

Character   any kind of person that a script writer or actor makes up

Expressions   the showing of different feelings by moving the face and body in different ways

Identification   when you think that another person has qualities or traits like your own

Identity   the different qualities or traits a person has that makes that person what he or she is

Idol   a TV or move character you like a great deal

Discussion Ideas

Ask your child who his or her favorite TV character is, and why. Children may want to make a list of TV characters and put stars next to the characters that they like. Next, they can underline the characters that have some traits that are similar to their own. The following questions may be helpful: "In what ways are they like you? In what ways are they different from you? Is it fun to watch TV characters that seem similar to you? Do you think any of these characters could be called good or bad? Is it possible for a character to be both good and bad?"

Parents should make sure that their children name traits other than superficial characteristics such as strength, beauty, popularity, or humor. Examples of discussions of characters follow: What is Dr. Huxtable on the "Cosby Show" like? Does he seem like a typical father? At times he may be strict, why? Does he ever make a mistake? Why does he make us laugh? Alf and Willy don't seem to get along. What is there about Alf that bothers Willy? Does Willy like Alf? If so, why? How can you tell that Alf really likes the Tanners?

Discussions can precede or follow the viewing of a favorite program.

Suggested Readings

Parents may want to suggest books with characters that are similar to the children's favorite (or least favorite) TV characters.

The following books have been adapted for television, and the children may be interested in comparing the book characters with the TV characters. These books are usually available in school or local libraries.

Barrie, J.M. *Peter Pan*

Clymer, Eleanor *Luke Was There*

Dixon, Franklin W. *The Hardy Boys* series

Gates, Doris *Little Vic*

Mazer, Harry *Snow Bound*

Wilder, Laura Ingalls *Little House on the Prairie* series

These books are sixth grade or junior high level:

Baum, Frank L. *The Wizard of Oz*

Crane, Stephen *The Red Badge of Courage*

Haley, Alex *Roots*

Kerr, M.E. *Dicky Hocker Shoots Smack*

Taylor, Mildred *Roll of Thunder, Hear My Cry* (a Newbery Award Winner)

Activity 1

1. Name something that Jesse on "Full House" (or another character) would never do.

2. Complete analogies or compose analogies on the activity page.

3. Name someone from a book, or a friend or neighbor, who is like a favorite character. How are they alike?

4. We sometimes like characters who seem ideal because they can do things that we can't do. Name one, and list the traits that describe him or her.

5. Change a TV character to be more likeable.

6. Make up a character that you'd like to see on TV or to be with.

7. Draw a favorite TV character.

8. Compare characters in a book with the *same* characters on TV (see Suggested Readings).

9. Family Games:

   a. **Choosing Favorites.** Each family member says which character he or she would like to be and why. Family members discuss what they like or don't like about those characters.

   b. **Who Am I?** Each family member lists four traits or mannerisms of a TV character. Other family members try to guess who the character is.

Example: Dr. Samuels on "Head of the Class" could be described as bossy, rude, pompous, silly.

c. **Opposite Traits.** One family member names a trait of a favorite TV character. Other family members try to name a character with the opposite trait.

Example: Eddie on "Family Matters" is silly. Mr. Moore on "Head of the Class" is serious.

Activity 2

Characters We Love and Hate

Analogies show the way that different things are related to each other. Complete these analogies.

1. Popeye is to Olive Oyl as Mickey Mouse is to

   _____ .

2. Roseanne is to Dan as Harriet is to

   _____ .

3. Dr. Huxtable is to Vanessa as Mr. Seavers is to

   _____ .

4. Mike is to Ben as Becka is to _____ .

5. Jessica is to *Murder She Wrote* as Kate is to

   _____ .

6. Joey is to Nicole as Michael is to _____ .

Now try these:

1. Mr. Thatcher is to Corky as _____ is to

   _____ .

2. Arvid is to Eric is to _____ is to

   _____ .

CHAPTER NINE

TV Is Only Part of the Picture

Television is an unrealistic world inhabited by young, healthy, middle-class white people. While it is true that African-Americans, the elderly, foreigners, and handicapped people appear on television more than ever before, they are often cast in stereotypic and negative roles. Women in particular are depicted unrealistically. These misrepresentations create problems because most children assume that TV programs depict life as it is or the way it should be. All too often, then, it is possible for children to form their opinions about minority groups on the basis of television's inaccurate portrayals.

The purpose of this chapter is to teach children about stereotypes, so that they will understand that they should not generalize about people from the examples they see on TV. We examine the many stereotypes of families, police work, men's and women's roles, racial and ethnic groups, the elderly, and handicapped people in an attempt to teach children that we are all members of different groups which are neither good nor bad, but are an important part of the world we live in.

What You Need to Know

In many ways, television can be a wonderful teacher. It can show children what life is like for other people in our country, around the world, and throughout history. However, many children do not realize that most TV programs are made to entertain rather than to teach us, and they may not understand that a program can be realistic in some ways and very unrealistic in others.

Most children display a greater understanding of family programs, such as the "Cosby Show," than other shows. They may assume that these programs portray family life as it *should* be, but they realize—based on their own firsthand experiences— that real families have greater difficulties solving their various problems.

On the other hand, children may be less critical of programs that depict unfamiliar people and places. For example, police officers on TV are usually involved in suspenseful, dangerous activities. Many children, not realizing that real police officers rarely fight, develop a stereotypic picture of policemen continually chasing and shooting people.

Most of the television research in the area of stereotypes has concentrated on race and sex roles. Research during the 1960's and 1970's, for example, reported that there were relatively few nonwhite and female characters on television. Only one-third of all TV characters were women, and most were in the smallest, least important parts. Nonwhites made up only 10 percent of all television characters, and they were also in the least significant parts. Both women and nonwhites tended to be portrayed in traditional, stereotypic roles, and were often depicted as dependent on or subordinate to white men. There were also very few TV characters (particularly females and blacks) under the age of sixteen or over the age of forty.

However, during the 1980's and 1990's there have been improvements for minorities. Most notably, the "Cosby Show," a program about a well-educated, affluent, African-American family, became one of the most popular talk shows on television, and the "Oprah Winfrey Show" became the most popular talk show. "Different World" broke new ground by portraying black college students, although most of the students are portrayed as silly rather than as serious.

Nevertheless, even today, blacks and other minorities tend to be in comedy programs, and are especially scarce in children's programs and daytime "soaps." Their portrayal on TV, in terms of both numbers and status, has remained relatively low. In addition, in news stories, African-Americans and Hispanics are portrayed more negatively than whites.

According to the National Commission on Working Women, the portrayal of women on TV has also improved since 1981. For example, their jobs have become more interesting and varied and the percentage of TV female characters who work is approximately the same as it is in the real world. This is a major change since the 1960's, when most women were portrayed as homemakers, and the 1970's when women were portrayed as either employed or mothers but not both.

However, men still tend to outnumber women on TV by three to one. Men outnumber women six to one on action/adventure shows, compared to only two to one on situation comedies.

Research studies have shown that television has far more power to influence children's attitudes than may have been previously believed. For example, when children watch programs that portray African-Americans favorably, their attitudes toward blacks become more positive, whereas programs that portray black people negatively will increase children's negative attitudes toward them. In another study, 40 percent of the white elementary school children surveyed stated that they learned about black people from television. In an instance such as this, it is impossible to ignore the impact of television on children's beliefs and attitudes.

In our research we found a clear relationship between the programs that children watch and the prejudicial attitudes that they express. For example, white children who watch more programs with major black characters are less prejudiced against African-American people. Our research was conducted at a time when there were no TV programs like the "Cosby Show," which presents a very positive, well-educated African-American family. However, even when programs include black characters who are somewhat silly or uneducated, if they are warm, caring people they will present a relatively positive image, especially for white children who know few black people.

In contrast to these findings, children who watch more violent television programs (which often portray blacks as villains or victims) tend to be more prejudiced against black people. Although these programs may not *cause* prejudice, they may encourage and reinforce it. Unfortunately, a child often does not understand that these shows aim to be entertaining rather than educational. In fact, children may misunderstand the intent of realistic, higher quality programs: In one class that we studied, a child who had watched "Roots" asked why the black people did not want to drink at the white people's water fountain! It is discouraging that a program which was intended to teach people about racial prejudice could be so badly misunderstood by a child. This provides a good example of why it is important for parents to watch TV programs with their children and encourage them to ask questions.

Despite the improved portrayals of female TV characters in recent years, new stereotypes are developing. The new, more liberated female television character is usually beautiful as well as competent. She may be over 30, or even 40, but as glamorous as Murphy Brown or Alexis Carrington. Characters such as Roseanne and her friends are the rare exceptions. If you compare female and male TV characters, you will find that the females are usually much younger and more attractive. It is discouraging to us that our research shows that elementary school girls admire the most beautiful female TV characters because of their looks, and not because of their other positive qualities. This suggests that TV programs may encourage girls to believe that beauty is the most important trait for women, even when they also try to convey the message that beautiful women can be competent as well.

TV also influences children's perceptions of appropriate goals for themselves. For example, a study that used commercials produced for research purposes found that 60-second commercials can influence children's career goals and attitudes. In this study, the commercials portrayed women talking about how they liked "ZING fruit drink" as well as their jobs. Some of the commercials showed a woman in such nontraditional roles as a butcher, pharmacist, welder, or laborer; the other commercials showed a woman as a telephone operator, fashion model, file clerk, or manicurist. The findings showed that the commercials influenced the children's career preferences, as well as their attitudes concerning appropriate careers for men and women. If a 60-second commercial has this influence, it seems likely that weekly programs are even more powerful in "teaching" children about appropriate sex roles.

In our research we also found a relationship between television viewing and sex prejudice. Girls who watched more game shows and programs that depict women as extremely silly or incompetent (such as reruns of "I Love Lucy" or "I Dream of Jeannie") were more prejudiced against females than were their classmates. Again, these programs do not necessarily *cause* prejudice, but they may influence the girls' attitudes. Whereas adults may watch these shows and think they are funny, children may assume that the programs show how women *really are* or *should* behave. Parents need to explain to their children that characters like Lucy are not intended to be role models of appropriate behavior.

Few older women characters are portrayed on TV, and most that have been portrayed have been rather negative. "The Golden Girls" and "Murder She Wrote" were the first programs to star older women and portray them as interesting and vibrant. Since children have distorted perceptions of age, television's failure to portray elderly people functioning normally as grandparents, neighbors, friends, or coworkers encourages children to assume that older people are unimportant and very different from the rest of the population. In addition, the portrayal of handicapped people as unhappy or disturbed individuals whose lives revolve around their problems tends to reinforce any fears a child has about people who are "different."

The role of Benny, a mentally retarded man on "L.A. Law," and Corky, a teenager with Down's syndrome on "Life Goes On," are major breakthroughs, because they portray retarded people living satisfying lives on a weekly program. However, these are still rare exceptions, and there are no similar portrayals of other kinds of handicapped children or adults on regularly scheduled programs.

It has taken television producers a long time to include more positive female characters and minority group characters on television, and even today, television presents only part of the picture. TV portrays working women, but they are usually glamorous and rarely in ordinary jobs. Very few programs portray retired people or handicapped people as main characters or as people living full and interesting lives. And, unfortunately, there are many reruns and old movies on TV that present very stereotypic characters. Parents can modify television's potentially negative impact on children by talking to them about television's stereotypes and omissions.

Special Words and Ideas
for Children to Review

American Indian or **Native American**   these are two names for the people who lived in America before the settlers came from Europe. Many Native Americans still live in America

Prejudice   to judge people before you know them, or to already have ideas about them

Stereotypes   the preconceived ideas we have when we think about a person

---

Discussion Ideas

1. TV does not always give us an accurate picture of what life is like. Ask your child to think of a program about a family that is different from your family. It may be helpful to discuss this just before or after watching a family program like the "Cosby Show," or "Roseanne."

2. Discuss the fact that most of the important TV characters are usually boys or men, and these males are usually young adults, white, and healthy. TV used to have almost no women stars or black stars, but this is changing. Can your child name some women TV stars? Black stars? White male stars? Compare the number in each category. Ask children to name famous African-American males. Can they name some who are not sports stars or entertainers?

3. Not all people are like the ones we see on TV. Children know that not all classes are like the students on "Head of the Class." Ask your child: "Are all white children like Doogie Howser, M.D.? How do we know?" Talk about the similarities and differences. Ask: "Are all black teen-agers like the stars of the "Cosby Show" or "Different World?" How do we know? Are all women as silly as Lucy ("I Love Lucy") or Corky Sherwood ("Murphy Brown")? How do we know? Explain the word *stereotype*.

4. Pretend that you and your child are visitors from outer space, and you only know about the United States from watching TV. What would you know about each of these?
   unattractive women
   handicapped people who live normal lives
   accents (regional: southern, midwestern, New York, Boston; foreign)
   police officers
   children who are mentally retarded
   American Indians or Native Americans
   poor people
   grandparents
   Asian people

5. Talk with your child about what we know about aliens from watching Alf. Are all aliens like Alf? How do we know? Are aliens from outer space real or are they make-believe, just as fairy tale or cartoon characters?

Suggested Readings

These books are available in many school and public libraries.

Ethnic Groups: Fiction

Gates, Doris *Little Vic*. A black boy trains a racing horse. The issue of prejudice is raised.

Greene, Bette *Philip Hall Likes Me. I reckon Maybe*. A story of a southern black girl. (Newberry Award)

Lexau, Joan *Striped Ice Cream*. An eight-year-old black girl and her family.

Myers, Walter Dean *The Young Landlords*. A group of grade school friends buy an apartment building for one dollar. (Coretta Scott King Award; pre-teen level)

Taylor, Mildred *Roll of Thunder, Hear My Cry*. A story of black children in the South. (Newberry Award; sixth-grade level)

McCabe, Inger *A Week in Henry's World: El Barrio*. Photographs and text of el barrio.

Ethnic Groups: Nonfiction

Brahs, Stuart *An Album of Puerto Ricans in the U.S.*

Lathan, Frank *The Rise and Fall of "Jim Crow."* The black struggle for equality in America.

Lester, Julius *To Be a Slave*

Butwin, Frances *The Jews in America*

Kurtis, Arlene *The Jews Helped Build America*

Wytrwal, Joseph *The Poles in America*

Dowdell, Dorothy and Joseph *The Japanese Helped Build America, The Chinese Helped Build America*

Stanek, Muriel *How Immigrants Contributed to Our Culture*

Reit, Seymour *Child of the Navajos.* A contemporary story of a nine-year-old Navajo boy.

Wiesenthal, Eleanor and Ted *Let's Find Out About Eskimos*

Male and Female Roles: Fiction

Merriam, Eve *Mommies At Work.* A picture book of the work mothers do at home and in the labor force.

Merriam, Eve *Daddies At Work.* A picture book of the work fathers do at home and in the labor force.

Traves, Isabella *Not Bad For a Girl.* The story of a girl who wants to join a Little League team.

Thomas, Marlo *Free to Be . . . You and Me.* A collection of short stories, poems, and songs.

Male and Female Roles: Nonfiction

May, Julian *Amelia Earhart: Pioneer of Aviation*

Warren, Ruth *Pictorial History of Women in America* (fifth-grade level)

Handicapped

Lasker, Joe *He's My Brother.* The story of a boy with learning disabilities.

McGrath, Edward *An Exceptional View of Life.* Short stories and poems by handicapped children.

Swarthout, Glendon and Kathryn *Whales to See.* A story about a class of children with learning disabilities.

Wolf, Bernard *Anna's Silent World.* A picture book about a deaf girl.

Activity 1

1. Be a stereotype detective. Find a stereotypic character on commercials or TV programs. What are the exaggerated characteristics that make him or her seem like a stereotype instead of a real person?

Clues: clothes, accent, facial expressions, gestures, behavior.

a black teen-ager who acts ridiculous
a helpless or childish woman
an ugly "bad guy"
a "dumb blond"
a "he-man" (who is very strong and never cries or fails)
a helpless old man or woman
a pathetic handicapped person
a "goody-goody" cute boy or girl
a smart person with glasses

These are types of characters who aren't on TV (in commercials or programs) very often. Can you find any examples of these?

a smart *and* athletic teen-ager
a serious African-American man
a physically handicapped person who lives a relatively normal life
an honest politician
a working grandmother or grandfather

2. How can we recognize a stereotypic character?

   Clues: clothes (including aprons, glasses, etc.), the way they they talk (accents, expressions, special words), behaviors and activities, gestures and physical expressions.

   Find examples on the TV programs that you watch.

3. Read a book about someone who is not like the TV characters in his or her group, or a book about people you don't see on TV very often. Some examples are in the suggested readings section of this lesson.

4. Draw a person in a nonstereotypic role. For example, a man ironing, a woman doctor, a black newspaper reporter.

5. Be a reporter: Interview five- to six-year-old children in your neighborhood.

   What do boys want to be when they grow up?

   What do girls want to be when they grow up?

6. Activity page: Match the different groups with the examples shown.

Activity 2

When TV is Only Part of the Picture

All people are members of different groups, even if they don't think about it. Match up the names of the characters with the groups that they're in, by drawing lines between the characters and the groups. Most characters represent more than one group. Try to use a different color crayon or pencil for each group.

Group	*Character*
Grandparents	Kevin Arnold ("Wonder Years")
Teenagers	Doogie Howser, M.D.
Italian-Americans	Dr. Huxtable
Males (men and boys)	Jesse ("Full House")
White people	Becky Conner ("Roseanne")
Black people	Alf
Females (women and girls)	Roseanne
Someone from Melmac	Theo Huxtable
Fathers	Carla (Cheers)
Mothers	Mrs. Tanner (Alf)

CHAPTER TEN

Violence and Action on TV

Have you ever noticed children imitating some of the action they have seen on television? Sometimes this may involve just make-believe "galloping" on an imaginary horse, driving an imaginary car, or "shooting" with pointed fingers at invisible pursuers. Often, however, if the violence they've witnessed is very realistic, children may also imitate punching or kicking. Since children can't pull their punches as well as TV actors they may occasionally hurt their brothers, sisters, and friends, and provoke a real fight. Those children who watch many violent action shows may begin to adopt some of the mannerisms and provocative attitudes of superheroes or police detectives and resort increasingly to fighting with their friends to settle the inevitable disagreements that arise among playmates.

In the past two decades, a growing number of social scientists, educators, mental-health specialists, and parents have been concerned that the considerable amount of violence on television may have a harmful impact on young viewers. Such concerns are not exaggerated, we believe. After all, children grow up watching huge amounts of television daily. From network programming they learn about other countries and different commercial products, and they imitate speech patterns, phrases, and songs. Obviously, they are likely to emulate certain types of aggressive actions from the many incidents of violence they see everyday on television. The children we questioned (in the study in which these lessons were tested) reported that they often imitated TV car chases on their bicycles or some of the fighting tricks they'd seen on TV. They also indicated that they occasionally got into arguments within the family by imitating attitudes or aggressive actions they'd seen on favorite TV programs.

It would be foolish to attribute all the violence in America to the influence of television. After all, there was plenty of violence in the country well before the introduction of TV. But even if television affects just 10 percent of all children by increasing their aggressiveness, it is still influencing many thousands every day. While most of the prime-time violent programming (including shows such as "Wise Guy," "China Beach," and "Midnight Caller") is shown later in the evening, some crime dramas are shown in the early evening when most children are watching TV. In addition, TV films and daily reruns on many local stations continue to be full of explicit violence, and they are often broadcast at times when children are very likely to be watching.

While we believe the networks and local stations have a responsibility to curb violent programming, the ultimate responsibility for limiting children's exposure to violence on TV rests with parents and other adult caretakers. The purpose of this chapter is to provide suggestions for teaching children that most violence on TV and in movies is not real and should not be imitated. We focus on explaining to children why violence is not fun, and on discussing other ways besides aggression to resolve the inevitable problems that arise in daily life.

Another purpose is to teach your children that the violence portrayed on TV is sometimes distorted, and that violence on

TV often seems fun or exciting because the consequences of violence are not usually shown on TV. It will also help you teach your children that there are other ways of solving problems that are preferable to violent confrontations.

What You Need to Know

According to George Gerbner and his colleagues at the University of Pennsylvania, the level of violence in prime-time television measured over twenty years has remained at about five violent acts per hour, although the number is much higher (20–25 acts per hour) on children's Saturday morning programs.

Of course, the violence is even higher on some prime-time programs. According to the National Coalition on Television Violence, there are an average of 25 violent acts per hour on "Alien Nation" and 37 per hour on "Hunter." Other programs are even more violent, and the "America's Most Wanted" program was rated the most violent of all with 53 violent acts per hour.

Does violent television programming increase the likelihood that children will engage in more fighting and disruptive behavior? For years many parents and even some mental-health specialists believed that watching violence on TV had little effect on children and might even be good for them, since it served to "drain off" some of their aggressive energy. The extensive research conducted by Professors Albert Bandura of Stanford University and Leonard Berkowitz of the University of Wisconsin has demonstrated quite clearly, however, that both children and adults exposed to violence in movies and TV rarely become *less* aggressive; rather, the evidence is fairly strong that they show *greater* tendencies to be aggressive after watching violent shows.

The studies we've just mentioned were carried out in university settings, and some social scientists and television network representatives have argued that real-life TV viewing may not produce the same results. However, a very important long-term study was completed by a group of investigators led by psychologists Monroe Lefkowitz, Leonard Eron, and L. Rowell Huesmann in upstate New York. They found that boys who had been watching many violent TV shows at age eight were rated as more aggressive by their friends and neighbors ten years later when they were eighteen, and were involved in serious criminal behavior when they were thirty. By careful statistical methods, the researchers showed that other factors (such as preference by already aggressive children to watch violent programming, family background, or social class) could not explain away this relationship. The results were clear: The heavy viewing of action shows influenced these children to become more aggressive as they grew up.

Leonard Eron, a professor of psychology at the University of Illinois, repeated this experiment with third and fifth grade children in Chicago. He found that girls as well as boys show similar effects of viewing heavy violence, a finding explained perhaps by the increased number of tough, fighting women on TV programs like "Hunter" or "Mancuso, FBI."

A large-scale study (sponsored by CBS) was conducted in England by Professor William Belson. Of 1,500 adolescent boys studied, 188 indicated they had engaged in at least ten or more acts of considerable violence in the previous six months. It turned out that the boys' tendencies to engage in serious acts of violence were particularly related to their intensive viewing of action shows on TV. Belson reported that the programs most related to the boys' increased violence were (1) shows depicting people involved in close relationships who attack one another and other persons; (2) Westerns which feature saloon brawls and fistfights; (3) fictional violence shows with very realistic fight scenes; (4) shows that depict violence as a desirable way to serve a good cause; and (5) programs which use violence for no discernible purpose.

Some of the most persuasive research results are from studies comparing children's behavior before and again two years after television was introduced in their town. Compared to "before TV" the children became more physically and verbally aggressive after TV became available.

After studying children in five countries (US, Australia, Finland, Israel and Poland) researchers have concluded that viewing TV violence leads to aggression, and that aggressive tendencies lead to viewing TV violence. Regardless of how it is studied, children and adults who watch more violent programs tend to behave more aggressively and to favor the use of aggression to resolve conflicts.

At the Yale University Family Television Research and Consultation Center we conducted one of the first studies which examined the relationship between TV viewing at home and the behavior in school of children as young as three and four years of age. In one investigation we found that boys and girls from middle-class backgrounds who were the heaviest TV viewers in this sample, and especially those who watched action shows, were more likely to get into fights and disrupt others' games in the nursery school. As in the Eron study, the viewing of action shows more likely caused this aggression and did not simply reflect a viewing preference by already troublesome children. These findings were further confirmed in a subsequent study we carried out with 200 children from blue-collar and lower socioeconomic family backgrounds. When we looked more closely into the family-life patterns of our children through home interviews, we found that those preschoolers who showed the most aggressive behavior over a year's time came from intact, rather conventional families who allowed the *child* to control the TV set and who had few outside interests, relying on heavy TV viewing as a social outlet.

In the project with elementary school children on which the present lessons are based, we also looked at the effects of TV viewing on behavior in school. We asked the teachers to rate their third, fourth, and fifth graders on a variety of classroom behaviors and personality traits. Although we didn't find a relationship between television viewing and aggression in the classroom, we did find that those children who watched violent programs with actors playing fantasy characters, like "Wonder Woman," were unhappy in class and had more difficulty in their interpersonal relationships. Although superhero programs are no longer popular on prime time TV, many are shown daily as syndicated reruns in the afternoon. It seems clear that watching violent programming, even fantasy programs, can have a harmful impact on children.

Since television continues to portray a great deal of violence, it is important to help children confront the nature of such action-packed programming. Research has shown that older children learn more about aggression from viewing than do younger children, who are more sensitive to constructive, prosocial programming. Boys also are more likely to imitate antisocial behavior from violent TV programs than girls. In our own study, we observed that the fathers who were heavy TV viewers had children who were likely to watch more action shows and spend less time reading. All of these results point again to the key role of parents' monitoring what's on TV and helping children understand violence in TV programs.

Children emulate undesirable attitudes as well as behaviors from watching violent TV. Many youngsters don't understand the cause-effect relations that lead to fights, and they come to

believe that violence is an easy, quick way of resolving problems. Since TV writers need to wind up a complex story in a
half hour or 60 minutes, they frequently use a shoot-out or
punch-out solution. Producers also believe that such rapid-fire
activities as fights and car chases will hold viewers' attention
so they won't change channels during the commercials which
continually interrupt the story. Unfortunately, young children
often lose track of the reasons for fights or the moral issues
involved in stories because of the rapid pace of programs and
the interruptions for advertising.

Children also need some help in dealing with the news. Many
acts of violence portrayed each night can be frightening to
young children. Action and violent scenes are the most visually
dramatic news stories, so newscasters tend to select them for
TV news programs. Our research found that nursery school
children who watched the news and action-detective stories,
and who were heavy television viewers, tended to be more
aggressive in school. Older children may not be as impression-
able, but even they (as well as adults) begin to develop false
assumptions about the amount of crime and violence that takes
place in the world. According to Professor George Gerbner of
the University of Pennsylvania, the news influences our attitudes about danger in the streets.

You can help children understand violence, and, to some
extent, inoculate them against imitation or misunderstanding
by pointing out some of the characteristics of action shows.
On TV programs you can call their attention to the way camera
techniques and background music intensify excitement. For
example, two characters may say to each other, "I've had
enough of you," and "I'm sick and tired of you." In real life,
that might be the end of the fight. But on TV, if the camera
zooms in on their faces, and if menacing music and the beat
of drums sound in the background, a much more violent fight

is likely to erupt. Television relies heavily on zooms, close-ups, and pounding music to excite viewers and warn them of increasing violence.

When a fight does erupt on TV, it is very often convincing, especially to children. Children often don't realize that actors purposely miss when they swing at each other, and that camera angles and sound effects are used to make the viewer think the fighting is real. You should explain to your child that these people are actors pretending to fight and they are well-trained in how to miss each other. After all, most actors are rather vain about their appearance and wouldn't want to end up with split lips, black eyes, or puffy cheeks.

American television doesn't often show the consequences of fighting or shooting. Characters are shot, fall down, and simply disappear from the plot and the screen. It's important to help children understand that real aggression doesn't solve a problem so easily. Instead, it is just the beginning of a problem, because if a person is hurt, he or she must spend days, weeks, or months recuperating. The aggressor also may hurt himself in hitting someone else. Also, if he shoots a person, he may feel terribly guilty afterward, and almost certainly would be arrested and stand trial, even if the shooting *was* in self-defense. Children should be told that policemen or detectives rarely resolve conflicts by shooting people, and if they do, they usually have to undergo a hearing to justify their resort to firearms. Children should also be urged to think about the families of persons shot or injured, who may suffer for years as a consequence. Children need frequent reminders of this in view of the continuous dosage of "easy" violence they get through television.

We've been talking so far of direct aggression, of persons hitting, strangling, or shooting each other, or engaging in destruction of property. There's also a good deal of verbal insult and "put-down" on television. A great deal of humor on situation comedies comes from insulting remarks such as Carla's putting down her friends on "Cheers," or Roseanne's teasing of her husband and children. To adults these seem harmless enough because we know people don't usually talk that way. Children often don't grasp this, especially since the laugh-track in the background makes such remarks sound funny. They need to see that to repeat many of the remarks heard on TV to other people would most likely hurt them deeply, and even provoke some real-life aggression. Parents can help children realize that we laugh at characters insulting each other on TV precisely because they're getting away with saying things we wouldn't say in real life.

Special Words and Ideas for Children to Review

Action-packed a TV program where a lot of things happen in a short time

Aggression (in context of this lesson) physical harm or threats to people or objects

Verbal Aggression spoken words, threats, insults

Bloodshed when people are hurt or killed in violent situations

Violence acts of cruelty involving physical pain or damage to people or property

Discussion Ideas

Action shows are shows which portray a lot of activity, such as car chases, fights, or people running to catch someone or to escape from someone. What action shows do you watch?

Read your child this violent passage from a TV script:

> An old blue car pulls sharply away from the curb with its brakes screeching, while someone jumps into the passenger seat and slams the door. The car quickly turns the corner and speeds away.
>
> A man starts his motorcycle on another street and begins to weave in and out of traffic. The blue car then pulls into an alley at high speed. The motorcycle turns into the same alley from the other direction. The blue car swerves as the motorcycle falls and skids into some trash cans. The blue car then speeds away.
>
> The motorcyclist gets up and pulls out a rifle from his pack, and quickly runs to the end of the alley, bends down on one knee, takes aim, and fires repeatedly at the blue car. The car is hit and immediately bursts into flames and crashes into a store.

Talk about how reading the above violent scene feels different than watching it on TV. The impact of special effects, music, imagination, etc., should be discussed.

Ask your child to think for a minute about how he or she feels when someone is hurt or killed in a TV program. Does it seem real? Stress that violence is not fun or funny. Ask if the real world is like that. Acknowledge that violence exists, but does not permeate the real world to the extent that television would have us believe. Talk about why there are so many violent TV programs.

Do the stars of TV programs ever get badly hurt or killed? Why or why not?

Parents can explain the concept of verbal aggression. Why is it portrayed as funny? Is it true that "sticks and stones may break my bones, but names will never hurt me?" Are there alternatives to verbal and physical aggression? Talk about how verbal aggression may seem funny on TV, but not in real life.

Sometimes people imitate verbal and physical aggression that they see on TV. Give examples from their own experiences. Ask your child: "Have you ever noticed yourself imitating violence on TV? Why does this happen? What can we do to stop it?"

Suggested Readings

Golding, William *Lord of the Flies*

Hall, Lynn *Troublemaker*

Hinton, Susan E. *The Outsiders*

Holland, Isabel *Amanda's Choice*

Wojciechowska, Maia Rodman *The Hollywood Kid*

Activity 1

1. Choose an action show and a cartoon that you usually watch, and keep track of the violent actions on the *Physical Aggression Chart* (Activity Page).

2. Choose a situation comedy that you usually watch, and keep track of the verbal aggression on the *Verbal Aggression Chart* (Activity Page).

3. After watching a TV show that seems violent, write down how you feel.

4. How can you tell the difference between violence on the news and violence on action programs?

5. Interview a real police officer. Ask him or her whether police work is as exciting in real life as it is on TV.

6. Draw two pictures where two people are solving a problem: One is violent and the other is not.

Activity 2

Physical Aggression Chart

Some cartoons and "action programs" show a lot of chasing, fighting, and bloodshed. If you watch a cartoon or action program, rate how much physical aggression was on the program by answering the following questions.

Name of program: _____

1. How many characters were killed on this program? _____

2. How many characters were physically hurt (but not killed)? _____

3. Were there any crimes committed on this show? _____ If there were, what were they? _____

4. Were there any car chases?

   Were there any car accidents? _____

   Were there any fires? _____

   Were there any other accidents or disasters? _____

   Name them:

5. How was the bad person punished?

6. Did the program make physical aggression seem fun or funny or exciting? _____

   Did it show that violence hurts people unfairly?

7. Sometimes programs show violence that seems wrong or silly because it was not necessary. Could the fighting or killing have been avoided by talking? Could the person have been arrested quietly instead of being chased in a car?

   _____

   _____

   _____

   _____

   _____

   _____

Activity 3

Verbal Aggression Chart

Some action programs show people saying mean things to each other, even if they don't fight. Some situation comedies show people making fun of each other by calling each other names or saying mean things about each other. These are examples of verbal aggression.

If you watch a program with verbal aggression, rate the program by answering the following questions:

Name of program: _____

1. What kind of verbal aggression was used on this program?

   a. People said mean things to each other, as if they wanted to hurt the other person physically (for example, "I'll knock you down" or "I'd like to hit you.")

   b. People made fun of each other, calling names or using other verbal put-downs.

2. Can you give an example of verbal aggression from this program?

   _____

   _____

3. Did the program make verbal aggression seem fun or funny or exciting? How?

   _____

   _____

   _____

4. How would you have felt if someone said something like that to you or about you?

_____

_____

_____

Activity 4

Different Ways of Solving Problems

FISTFIGHT

Look at the following three pictures. The picture below shows two people fighting the way characters on TV often fight. There are also two pictures on the next page. They show what might happen later, after the fight. Which one of these things do you think would happen in real life?

FISTFIGHT

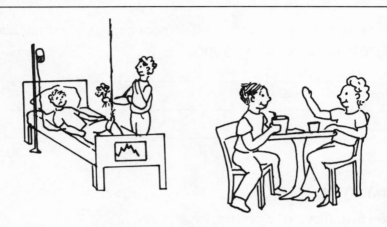

GUNFIGHT

Now look at this problem. The picture on top shows two men fighting with guns the way characters on TV often fight. The two pictures on the bottom show what might happen later, after the fight. Which one of these things do you think would happen in real life?

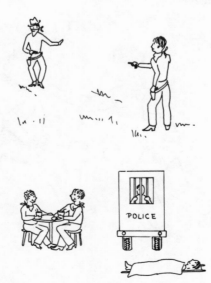

FIGHT OVER TOYS

Here are three pictures again. The picture on top shows two girls wanting to play with the same toy. The pictures on the bottom show two things that the girls can do. Which do you think is the better thing to do?

SOLVING FRUSTRATING PROBLEMS

These pictures present children in frustrating situations. After completing this chapter, look at each picture separately. Ask your child, "Has something like this ever happened to you?" "What did you do when this happened?" "If this hasn't happened to you, what would you do if it ever did?" "What do you think *this* boy/girl will do?" "What kinds of things can they say or do to make things better?"

CHAPTER ELEVEN

Commercials and the Television Business

All parents are aware of the powerful influence that television commercials have on their children. For many years, TV advertisers have produced commercials that are designed to attract and hold the attention of children of all ages. There has been increasing controversy regarding whether these commercials are fair, since they are intended to persuade children who are not mature enough to evaluate critically the messages presented. Groups such as Action for Children's Television (ACT) have been especially vocal in their complaints that TV commercials teach children poor nutritional habits and generally encourage the view that having possessions will make a person happy and popular. Perhaps most annoying to parents are commercials' underlying message that parents who love their children will buy them the wonderful products being advertised.

Many parents with whom we have spoken express frustration with the persuasive power of TV commercials, and they find it difficult to deal with their children's repeated requests for food and toys that they've seen advertised. Although research has shown that advertising strongly influences a child's desire for various products, parents can still modify their children's response to commercials. Our experiences with third, fourth, and fifth graders have shown us that children can learn to be less susceptible to television commercials. Although as children mature they tend to become increasingly skeptical about commercials, it is only when they understand the purposes of advertising and the techniques that are used to enhance products that they can critically evaluate what the commercials actually say, what they leave out, and what they subtly imply. Many of the special effects and other television production techniques that were discussed in previous chapters are directly relevant to the understanding of commercials.

The purpose of this chapter is to provide basic information about why there are commercials on TV, the different kinds of commercials, and how children can learn to view television commercials critically. We hope that some of our suggestions may also be helpful to adult readers who, too often, are not as analytic about TV commercial messages as they ought to be.

What You Need to Know

The word *commercial* is short for *commercial message*. Every hour on television is carefully planned to have enough minutes for these "messages." By selling commercial minutes to advertisers, TV station owners are able to defray the costs of their programs. It is very expensive to advertise on television (many thousands of dollars for every half minute), but commercials are still a bargain for advertisers. Sending a letter to a thousand people would cost $250 for postage alone. So, if an advertiser wants to reach a large audience, TV advertising costs less money, and it lets advertisers talk about and visually portray their products.

Children watch an average of 19,000 to 20,000 commercials each year. Most parents assume that their children understand the purpose of advertising, but research has shown that young children cannot even distinguish between commercials and television programs. Communication specialists Scott Ward, Daniel Wackman, and Ellen Wartella have conducted studies of several hundred children in kindergarten, third, and fifth grades. They found that the majority of the kindergartners did not know what a TV commercial was, although many were able to describe the fact that commercials were shorter than programs. These children did not understand why commercials were shown on TV or what they were attempting to do. The third and fifth graders were more knowledgeable, but even they did not fully understand the purpose of commercials. The persuasive power of television commercials was demonstrated in a study of preschool children who accompanied their mothers to the supermarket. Psychologists Joann Paley Galst and Mary Alice White at Teachers College, Columbia University found that children who watched more commercial television programs made more requests for purchases while shopping in the supermarket with their mothers. On the average, the children attempted to influence their mothers' purchases once every two minutes. The most heavily requested products were sugared cereals and candy which are frequently advertised in commercials directed at children. What is surprising is that the children also attempted to influence many of their mothers' other purchases, including dishwashing and laundry detergents. We would not expect children to be particularly interested in these products, so it seems likely that their requests can be attributed to the heavy advertising of detergents on daytime television.

Television commercials may also encourage materialistic attitudes. In a study conducted by researchers at McGill University, four- and five-year-old children were asked whether they would prefer to play with a "not so nice" boy who has a toy barn or a "nice" boy who does not have the toy. Children who had seen the toy advertised were twice as likely to prefer to play with the "not so nice" boy who had the toy.

Many commercials hint that a product will make a person happier or more popular. In a study by Bruce Shaak and his colleagues, second and fifth graders were shown a commercial for cookies. In one version of the commercials, a child was shown winning new friends by giving out the cookies; in the other version the child did not win new friends. Children who saw the commercial where the child gained new friends were more likely to show an increased preference for the cookies. This commercial was especially persuasive for the fifth graders.

For many years, popular characters from TV programs were made into dolls or toys that were especially popular with children who watched those programs. However, "program length commercials" are a new concern to parents of young children. These refer to programs that were developed to promote a particular toy or doll *after* that toy or doll was already for sale. These programs are often of mediocre or poor quality, but they attract an audience because of their connection with the toys. The programs are frequently little more than a 30- or 60-minute commercial for that toy, even though the program is interrupted for other commercials as well.

The Federal Trade Commission (FTC) is the government agency that is responsible for regulating television commercials. The FTC has been actively involved in the controversy about TV advertising directed at children. The amount of time devoted to commercials on children's TV has ranged from 9–12 minutes each hour during the last decade. Action for Children's Television (ACT), a public interest group, has petitioned the FTC to regulate these commercials more effectively, especially those for candy and other sugared products. In 1978 the FTC stated that it is "unfair and deceptive" to address commercials for any product to children who are too young to understand the selling purpose of commercials. In 1979, ACT demanded that commercials be banned from children's television programs. The networks claimed that this would make children's television programs financially impossible.

The situation soon got worse instead of better. President Reagan's deregulation efforts in 1984 resulted in an increase in advertising of an additional 1.5 minutes each hour of children's programs. In recent years, Congress has again questioned whether commercials aimed at children, including "program-length commercials" should be more restricted or even completely banned.

This debate will probably continue. However, even if commercials were banned from children's television programs, children would still be exposed to many commercials during their after-school and prime-time television viewing.

In Chapter 6, we talked about some of the effects that are used on TV to make things look better than they really are. Many of those same effects are used in commercials. For example, if you look closely at a pizza commercial, you can see how the light shines on the sauce and cheese, making it look moist and chewy. Advertisers sometimes use slow motion to make the melted cheese drip slowly off the knife. It looks so good you can almost taste it. And that's the idea the commercial is trying to present—the viewer will remember that image when he or she sees the product at the supermarket, or will order it at a fast food restaurant.

There are other camera and lighting effects that commercials often use. For example, toys are sometimes held close to the camera with no children nearby, which makes the product seem bigger than it really is. Special lighting, music, and sound effects can also be used to make toys seem more attractive. Editing can also be used to make advertised products seem more exciting. For example, a commercial for a toy rocket might edit together tapes of many children looking excited and happy with a tape of the rocket going into space.

When children watch commercials on TV, it's important for them to understand that these ads have one purpose: They want the viewer to remember the product and then to buy it. Help your child to see how the advertisers hint at other ideas in order to persuade them to buy. For example, commercials for candy or food may show people eating and having fun with their friends. When children (and adults) see these commercials, it gives the impression that the product being advertised is especially delicious and fun to eat.

Sometimes commercials use television characters or celebrities to endorse the product being advertised. Celebrities are banned from children's commercials, but children may be influenced by celebrities in other commercials. Research by Andrew Iskoe has shown that these celebrities are very effective in persuading children to desire a product. In Iskoe's study of first, third, and fifth graders, popular celebrities increased children's preferences for the product advertised up to 67 percent. When commercials like this appear on TV, parents should talk to their children about the implications involved. For example, when Michael Jackson advertises a soft drink, children should understand that the use of that product will not make them as talented or famous as Jackson. Or when commercials advertise medicine by filming the scene in front of the Capitol in Washington, D.C., children should realize that the U.S. government is not endorsing the product. Of course, these commercials are not *overtly* stating these misrepresentations, but they certainly are hinting at them.

It's against the law to lie on a commercial, and there are rules that advertisers must follow. For example, bread and cereal commercials which promise that their products build muscles or improve athletic ability have been banned. But hints are often legal, and may be very effective. Recently, the claims of some breakfast cereals and other foods that they prevent heart disease have been criticized by health experts, and Congress has asked the Food and Drug Administration (FDA) to respond to its demands to prevent such misleading claims

Another example can be found in toy commercials. When several toys are advertised at the same time, the National Association of Broadcasters' Codes require that written or spoken disclaimers say "Each sold separately." Unfortunately, not all children understand that this means each toy must be bought by itself. Parents need to explain to their children that buying all the toys depicted in one commercial can add up to a lot of money, even if each toy is relatively inexpensive. Other disclaimers that may not be understood by children are "assembly required" and "batteries not included." However, if the disclaimers are worded more simply (for example, "You will have to buy the batteries yourself") young children are much more likely to understand the message.

Children should also learn about *political advertisements,* since they see them every year at election time. Explain to your child that these advertisements try to get the viewers to vote for someone, instead of telling them to buy something. Point out how these commercials may use some of the same effects that are used to advertise products. For example, if a commercial shows a crowd of people cheering for the candidate, that makes us think that many people are voting for the candidate and so we should, too.

There are other short messages on TV besides commercials, called *public service announcements*. As a special service to the people watching, these announcements are intended to tell them something that is in the public interest. You can point out examples of public service announcements, such as those against drugs, or asking us to give money to a charity.

Television stations that show commercials are called *commercial television stations*. Some of the money the stations receive for showing commercials goes to pay for the programs that we see, and the rest of the money goes to the station itself. The more people that watch the programs on a commercial station, the more the advertiser has to pay to show the commercial. That means more money for the commercial station. Since the commercial station can make more money from a program that more people watch, only the most popular programs will stay on the air.

There's another kind of TV station called a *public television station*. The money for their programs comes from the government and from donations made by corporations and by the viewers. There are no commercials on public television, although after a program, major contributors are listed. A few days each year, the station asks viewers for contributions. "Mister Rogers' Neighborhood," "Sesame Street," "3–2–1 Contact," "Wonderworks," and "Degrassi High" are popular children's programs on public television.

The most important point is to teach your children that commercials tell people to buy what the advertiser is selling, and that showing commercials brings money for programs and additional money for commercial TV stations. Help your children to be aware of what the advertiser wants them to buy and to decide for themselves if it's something they really want or need. Encourage them to think about the actual merits of the product, and to look for ways that special effects are used to make things look bigger than they really are, or better, or more fun.

Special Words and Ideas for Children to Review

Advertise   to make a product known to people so that they will remember it and want to buy the product

Advertisement   preparing a product to be advertised on TV in a way that will make it look better than any other product of the same type

Brand loyalty   when a person keeps buying a product because of the brand name

Commercials   advertisements on TV. Commercials help pay for the TV programs.

Market   the people that a network or local TV station can reach with its broadcast signal who might buy a product that is advertised

Profit   a profit is the money made when a product is sold for a higher price than it cost to make. Networks and local TV stations make profits by selling broadcast time to sponsors for more money than the TV program cost to make.

Product   the item that is being advertised on a TV commercial

Selling time   Networks and local TV stations sell time (usually 10, 30, or 60 seconds) to advertisers in order to pay for the cost of TV programs. The cost of buying commercial time depends upon the size of program audience and how much time the advertiser wants to buy. Usually one tries to buy advertising time on several different programs or time slots.

Sponsor A sponsor helps pay for the cost of a TV program so that it can advertise its product during the broadcast.

Discussion Ideas

Ask your child if he or she ever bought anything because it looked good on TV. How was it different than was expected? Was that fair? What can we do about it?

Go over the four types of advertisements, using the table below. (Ages eight to twelve) Try to point out an example of each when you watch television with your child.

1. *Commercials:* These advertisements pay for the programs, which cost a lot of money to make. Commercials can try to sell any kind of product.

2. *Political advertisements:* These talk about a person running for an elective office and try to convince people to vote for him or her. The candidate pays the network for the time, so these also help pay for the TV programs.

3. *Promotional advertisements:* A network or station will advertise programs in order to attract a larger audience. Programs that are popular can charge more for commercials.

4. *Public service announcements* (PSA): The government tells the networks that they must show these announcements for free. A PSA will give information or try to change people's ideas and behaviors. Examples include anti-drug or anti-smoking messages.

Using the chart below, go over the techniques used in advertising to make products seem better than they really are. (Ages seven to twelve)

Advertising Techniques	*Advertising Effects*
1. Close-up	makes product look larger
2. Sound effects	makes product seem more fun or exciting
3. Special lighting	makes product look more attractive
4. Including additional toys or accessories	makes product seem more fun or exciting
5. Product shown with happy people	makes it look as though everyone enjoys the product
6. Music or songs	helps you remember the product
7. Attractive people using product	makes it seem as if using the product makes you attractive or popular
8. Celebrity talks about product	makes it seem as if using the product makes you attractive or popular
9. Toy shown without any people nearby	makes product look larger
10. Written information such as "batteries not included"	makes the message seem less important if announcer does not also give the same information

Suggested Readings and Viewing

"Buy Me That!", a documentary revealing the tricks used in TV commercials, was produced by *Consumer Reports* and has been telecast on HBO.

Research on the Effects of Television Advertising on Children, a report prepared for the National Science Foundation is a good review that is recommended for parents.

A pamphlet, *Children's Advertising Guidelines*, is available from the Children's Advertising Review Unit, National Advertising Division, Council of Better Business Bureaus, Inc., 845 Third Avenue, New York, N.Y. 10022.

Activities

1. While watching TV during the weekend, use a chart like the one below to keep a record of number of commercials or amount of time used by commercials (All ages)

   a. How many TV commercials do you watch every day? Next time you watch TV, keep track of the number of commercials for a half-hour program (or for half of an hour program), by writing the name of each product that is advertised. (Also list commercials for political candidates).

   Name of program: _____

   Time that program begins: _____

   ### Name of Product

   1. _____
   2. _____
   3. _____
   4. _____
   5. _____
   6. _____
   7. _____
   8. _____
   9. _____

10. _____

11. _____

12. _____

13. _____

14. _____

15. _____

Time that program ends: _____

   b. How much time did you spend watching TV commercials? Next time you watch TV, use a watch or a clock with a second hand, and keep track of the number of minutes spent on commercials for a half-hour program (or half of an hour program). Write down the names of each product (or political candidate). It will help you to remember that most commercials are 15 seconds, 30 seconds, or 60 seconds.

   Name of program: _____

   Time that program begins: _____

   List all commercials and length of time for each:

Name of product	Length
_____	____ seconds
_____	____ seconds
_____	____ seconds
_____	____ seconds
_____	____ seconds

_____ ____ seconds

_____ ____ seconds

_____ ____ seconds

_____ ____ seconds

_____ ____ seconds

_____ ____ seconds

_____ ____ seconds

Time that program ends: ____

Total: ____ seconds = ____ minutes

2. Think of one commercial which made you think a product was better than it really was. Talk about the special effects or other techniques that were used. (All ages)

3. Write an advertisement about a product that would be hard to sell, that people usually would not be interested in buying, e.g., a shoe box, an empty bottle, a balloon. (All ages) a. Draw or paint illustrations to go with it. b. Act it out.

4. List the products on TV commercials which are related to beautifying people, e.g., makeup, shampoos, toothpaste, appliances. Which commercials are exaggerated? Which commercials are "honest" in presentation? (All ages)

5. List the products on TV commercials which are related to eating, e.g., food, drinks, candy. Which commercials are exaggerated? Which commercials are honest? (All ages)

6. List the products which relate to play, i.e., toys and games? Which commercials are exaggerated? Which commercials are honest? (All ages)

7. Write down the subject of a public service announcement or political advertisement that you saw on TV this week. (Ages eight to twelve)

9. Think of a way to reword or demonstrate one of the following messages so that all children would understand it: "Each sold separately," "Assembly required," "Batteries not included." (Ages eight to twelve)

10. Family Activity: Think of commercials that don't really tell us what a product is like. For example, what do Michael Jackson commercials tell us about the taste of Pepsi Cola?

CHAPTER TWELVE

You and TV: Who's in Charge

Throughout this book we've encouraged parents and children to discuss television programs with each other, and we've stressed the need for children to become more discerning, active television viewers. We go one step further in this chapter: Here we examine the ways that parents and children can work together to exert *their* influence over network programming. By expressing opinions about programs and commercials, by sending letters to networks, producers, and celebrities, and by being aware of laws and agencies that regulate the industry, viewers can wield their power to bring more appropriate and better quality programming to commercial television.

The major goals of this chapter are to help children understand their potential influence on TV programming and to learn to use TV reviews and schedules in order to watch the best programs.

What You Need to Know

In 1934 under the Federal Communications Act, Congress created the Federal Communications Commission (FCC) to set rules concerning who may broadcast on television and under what circumstances they may do so. Part of the FCC's duties are to allocate available space to public and commercial broadcasters and determine what rights and privileges they may have. The agency also concerns itself with cable television, pay television, and any other communication service. Television stations receive licenses from the FCC which must be renewed every three years. To maintain their licenses, stations must schedule news and community-affairs shows as well as entertainment programs. At least 90 days before its license expires, a station must file an application for renewal with the FCC. This application must include all the information concerning the station's past programming and future plans. The public can inspect this application at the station or at the Washington office of the FCC.

In 1974 the FCC adopted its *Children's Television Report and Policy Statement* establishing children's programming and advertising guidelines and standards for commercial television broadcasters. This statement emerged from a three-year rule-making proceeding that was influenced by public opinion and pressure groups composed of concerned parents and educators. The guidelines for programming dealt with three main issues; the need for diversified programs that are educational and cultural; the need for specific programming—particularly educational—geared to preschoolers and to school-aged children; and the need for a better-balanced scheduling of children's programs throughout the week, not just on Saturday morning.

The guidelines for advertising that were set forth in this statement specified that advertising in children's programs should be reduced to 9½ minutes per hour on weekdays, that separations between program content and commercial messages should be clear, that "host selling" of products (characters on a program promoting products) should be eliminated, and that "tie-ins" (where products are promoted within the body of the program) should be eliminated.

In October 1979 *A Report of the Children's Television Task Force* was issued to the FCC and made available to the general public. Briefly, the report stated that in the last ten years, very little new children's programming had been produced either for preschoolers or for the older children on public television. The report also noted that few local commercial stations had been willing to produce their own shows, and it concluded that broadcasters had not adequately met the guidelines of the 1974 Policy Statement. In December 1979 the FCC recommended that a certain amount of broadcast time should be set aside for children, specifically 2½ hours for school-age children and 5 hours for preschoolers during weekdays between 8:00 A.M. and 8:00 P.M.

This controversy over regulation, which involves the issues of free speech and freedom of the press, has been going on since the beginning of broadcasting.

In the 1980's, the Reagan Administration deregulation efforts resulted in the elimination of limits on advertising time or time for other "nonprogram" material on children's television. As a result, the amount of advertising has increased. Deregulation has also meant an increase in violent TV programs earlier in the evening, as well as increase from 19 to 26 violent acts each hour on children's TV programs from 1980 to 1990. In the last few years, Congress is again considering a legally required minimum amount of educational or information programs for children, and new legislation that could limit advertising and decrease TV violence.

Another government agency which regulates television, the Federal Trade Commission (FTC), serves to prohibit unfair and deceptive advertising on television. (As we mentioned in the previous chapter, there are also two independent organizations, the Children's Advertising Review Unit of the Better Business Bureau, and the National Association of Broadcasters, which have prepared guidelines for advertisers of products directed to children.) The main difficulty with both the FCC and FTC is their relative inability or unwillingness to enforce regulations. Rarely is a license revoked once it is granted, despite dramatic cases challenging television content that have come before the courts. One example was the case of fifteen-year-old Ronny Zamora, who killed an elderly woman in Florida. His attorney pleaded "involuntary television intoxication," and the family attempted to sue the three major networks, claiming that Ronny imitated negative behavior depicted on TV. The U.S. District Court in southern Florida dismissed the motion because no specific television program was cited as the stimulus for Ronny's robbery and murder of his victim.

In another instance, a nine-year-old girl, Olivia Niemi, was sexually assaulted in California by four youths. The child's lawyer claimed that the assailants got their idea from "Born Innocent," a graphic TV program aired three days before the assault on Olivia. The courts dismissed the case on the grounds that NBC's right to broadcast was protected by the First Amendment, and that there was no intent to incite violence. The network defended itself by stating that the program was a serious drama depicting some of the problems that take place in a girls' reformatory.

Even before such controversial and violent programs made headlines, public-interest groups had been active in influencing the networks and advertisers to produce better-quality programs and reduce the amount of violence portrayed—especially in programs directed to children. For example, Action for Children's Television (ACT) is continuously waging a campaign for quality programming as well as curtailment of advertising in children's programs. This group has succeeded in eliminating candy-vitamin advertising and has helped reduce violence on Saturday morning cartoon shows. A similar organization, the New York Council on Children's Television, has conducted conferences, workshops, and informal discussion groups to help parents encourage their children to become more selective, to urge parents and children to discuss programs together, and to help parents monitor their children's viewing.

The Council of Children, Media and Merchandising, formed in 1970, has been a watchdog for the public concerning commercials, especially those directed toward the children's market. One of their major concerns is the number of nutritionally poor foods advertised on television, such as candy, cookies, and sugar-cereals. This organization has taken a strong stand urging the Federal Trade Commission to be stricter regarding the enforcement of existing advertising codes involving children's programs.

It is important for children to know that TV programs are responsive to complaints and praise from viewers. You should encourage your child to write to producers, networks, the Federal Communications Commission, or managers of TV stations. Similarly, children should be urged to write to the FTC and to advertisers if they feel a particular commercial is unfair. Parents and children should also be aware of unsuitable scheduling practices. Many times an excellent children's program does not gain a large audience because stations broadcast those shows at times that conflict with a child's schedule. For example, the afternoon specials usually are planned for four o'clock, a time when many children are in after school care programs, taking music lessons, playing with friends, attending school club meetings, or participating in sports. Other quality children's programs are scheduled very early in the morning, at dinner time, or on Saturday afternoon, when children have other activities planned. You can help your child write a letter about these and other concerns. Some useful addresses are listed at the end of this chapter.

Parents can work together in a variety of ways to influence networks to broadcast more educational programming as well as programs geared to specific age groups. With other parents and groups such as a local ACT chapter, you can survey your community to find resources that will be useful. The Parent Teacher Association, church groups, Girl Scouts, Boy Scouts, and education associations such as the National Education Association, the American Association of School Administrators, and the National Association of Elementary School Principals have all been interested in the effect of television on children. With support from these organizations it might be possible to induce a local station to try out new programs that have appeared around the country. Keep informed through your newspaper or magazines about new children's programs. Urge your local station manager to at least investigate the possibility of a trial period. Help publicize good programs by letting other parents know of their existence. Unfortunately, not all people use a guide or newspaper listing to select their daily programs and instead just turn on the set, not knowing what is on.

It is also important to support the growth of public television in your community. These stations have been in existence since 1952 and are funded by the Corporation for Public Broadcasting and by annual fundraising. They have no advertising and can offer more specialized programs designed to reach children, the elderly, different ethnic groups, and people with special needs, such as the handicapped. There are public television stations in all fifty states.

Instructional Television (ITV) broadcasts are programs carried on public broadcasting stations designed to reach children in their schoolrooms. These educational programs are broadcast during school hours and cover a range of subjects. You might want to suggest that your school take advantage of these offerings. Each program is accompanied by written material for the teacher to use with the children to help enrich existing courses.

You might also suggest to your school librarian ways in which television can be linked to books. Here are some ideas:

- *A television bulletin board*—notices of future television programs having educational or positive social messages. Along with the notices, list related books. For pleasure-reading about television, post cartoons with captions. Make a cartoon scrap-book for children, filled with TV-related and book-related cartoons.

- *A "TV-tie-in table"*—Display books that relate to current or recent TV programs.

- *Books related to TV events*—Use attractive signs to show where a child can find materials related to sports events. Olympics and Super Bowl or World Series games should create an interest in reading fiction and nonfiction sports books.

- *Feature science books*—watch the science series on public television (such as "3–2–1 Contact"), post notices and display books on science and biographies of famous scientists.

- *Books about outer space, science fiction, and astronomy* can be tied in with programs such as "Star Trek" and "Alf."

- "The Big Blue Marble" program could be tied in with books about cultures and countries. Clip out newspaper items about different cultures around the world.

- *Books about TV*—Set up a special shelf of books describing the television industry, technical aspects of TV, and careers in television. This is a growing field for women.

- *Conversation hour*—Invite parents and children for afternoon or evening discussions comparing books to TV adaptations. Compare settings, characters, endings, etc. Which version is better—TV or the book? Lots of discussion should take place if the notices about the *Conversation Hour* include the time of the TV program, and if the books are made available for the participants to read before the discussion.

- *TV newsletters as part of library news*—circulate to children—let them know about library books that relate to TV. This could be a one-page newsletter to be sent home for parents to read, too. Have students submit TV reviews.

If you now review your child's TV viewing record (suggested in Chapter 4), and find that your child is not only watching too much TV, but is watching indiscriminately, there are some things you can do to remedy the situation. The most important way that children can "control" television is to carefully choose the programs that they watch by referring to a television guide or newspaper schedule. Show your child how to use these schedules. Encourage him or her to read any reviews or descriptions of programs.

The one recent development that is potentially the most important for helping parents and children take charge of television is the videocassette recorder (VCR). As we noted in chapter one, as of November, 1989, approximately 68.8% of American households owned at least one VCR, surpassing even the availability of cable. The VCR provides the opportunity to tape programs that are on too late or too early, or even at a time when no one is at home, so that they can be seen at a more convenient time. If parents are concerned about their child watching a particular program, they can tape it and "preview" it before permitting their child to watch it, or watch it together and discuss any parts that concern the parents or child.

VCRs also provide the opportunity to tape programs so that they can be watched again and again; or to stop and replay a segment if you want to understand it better; or even examine it to look for special effects or other techniques that we talked about in earlier chapters. Once a program is taped, commercials can be avoided with the "fast forward" button. Of course, VCRs can also be used to play favorite movies or educational programs that can be bought, rented or borrowed.

Parents can begin to develop their own VCR library. Good sources for reviews of videocassettes are daily newspapers or magazines that are directed to parents, such as *Parents' Choice,* a monthly magazine that is found in most libraries. In addition, *Parents' Choice* and *Consumer Reports* have published a *Guide to Video Cassettes for Children.* Libraries also lend videotapes and some even provide descriptions of their listings.

Unfortunately, many families do not take as much advantage of their VCRs as they expected to when they bought them. They may tape special movies or programs, but it is rare for a family to take the time at the beginning of the week to sit down with a weekly TV program guide to determine whether there are any programs that they want to tape. More than any other strategy, that could put the family truly in charge of the TV set. Of course, the examples that the parents set are very important. Our own research has shown that the most important influence on children's viewing habits is their parents' television viewing. Parents' viewing influences how much time the children spend watching TV, the types of programs that they watch, and their perception of television's importance in their lives.

The availability of VCRs also makes it feasible to offer television programs in the schools at times other than when regularly scheduled educational programs are transmitted via cable or satellite. This enables a teacher, just as it does a parent, to use selected shows for discussion. Science, drama, art and music on public television stations can be used to supplement print material in the classroom. Several teachers we know have also used segments from commercial television in order to make a point more dramatically than textbooks may provide.

Parents, teachers and children can discuss whether they have ever watched programs that they didn't really like—programs that weren't entertaining and didn't teach anything. Discuss self-regulation: Do your children watch TV even when they don't like the program? Encourage your child to set up *guidelines* for TV viewing and make a *schedule* for TV watching. We offer sample parent guides in the appendices.

Perhaps the most important ingredient in your family's television diet will be the *family discussion* period about program content. Our research indicates repeatedly that the parent, the teacher, or a group leader can make a difference in helping children understand a program and learn from it.

Special Words and Ideas for Children to Review

Criticize   to give your opinion of something after you've thought about it very carefully. This includes saying what you like and what you don't like.

Fair to be aware that there are good and bad things about a person or event

Influence to affect a person or thing without apparent force or direct authority

Interpret to explain the meaning of something

Law the rules of government that tell people what they must do or must not do

Unfair to say only good *or* bad things, to give only one side of an issue or event

Viewpoints your ideas about someone or something

Discussion Ideas

1. What techniques does TV use to influence your feelings about a a TV character? A real person? Be sure your child is aware of laugh-tracks, the responses of other characters, camera effects, and special effects.

2. Review the following important points we made in this book about how TV influences us:

   ■ TV can make something look better than it really is, such as a toy on a commercial

   ■ TV, through the use of camera techniques and special effects, can make impossible things seem real (for example, Alf, Big Bird).

   ■ TV can influence how you feel about a character by showing you how other characters respond to him or her.

   ■ TV can influence our ideas and feelings toward ourselves and people who are different from us.

- Special effects, music, lighting, camera techniques, laugh-tracks—all are used to help create a mood and affect our emotions.

- TV can influence us to act in either an aggressive or a cooperative manner.

- Television, with all of its many programs, is designed mainly to entertain the viewer.

3. Now, what can we do to *influence* TV? Ask your child if he or she has ever seen a TV program that he thought shouldn't be on TV. Help your child distinguish between programs and commercials that are bad or unfair and those that are uninteresting, possibly because they are intended for a younger or an older audience. Talk about schedules and guidelines for TV watching. What kinds of things could your child do instead of watching TV? Make a list of all the activities your child could do alone, or with the family.

Suggested Books for Parents and Educators

Cassata, M. & Skill T. (1983) *Life on a daytime television: Tuning-in American serial drama.* Norwood, NJ: Ablex.

Doerken, M. (1983). *Teaching television.* Englewood Cliffs, NJ: Educational Technology Publications.

Esserman, J.F. (1981). *Television advertising and children: Issues, research and findings.* New York: Child Research Service.

Greenfield, P.M. (1984). *Mind and media: The effects of television, videogames and computers.* Cambridge, MA: Harvard University Press.

Huesmann, L.R. & Eron, L.D. (1986). *Television and the aggressive child: A cross-national comparison.* Hillsdale, NJ: Erlbaum.

Jackson. A.W. (Ed.) (1982). *Black families and the medium of television.* Ann Arbor, MI: Bush Program in Child Development and Social Policy.

Kelley, M.R. (1983). *A parents' guide to television: Making the most of it.* New York: Wiley.

Postman, N. (1984). *Amusing ourselves to death.* New York: Viking.

Signorielli, N. (1985). *Role portrayal and stereotyping on television:* An annotated bibliography of studies relating to women, minorities, aging, sexual behavior, health and handicaps. Westport, CT: Greenwood Press.

Singer, D. G., Singer, J.L. & Zuckerman, D. M. (1981). *Getting the most out of TV.* Glenview, IL: Scott, Foresman.

Singer, D. & Kelly, H.B. (1984). *Parents, children and TV: A guide to using TV wisely.* Chicago, IL: The National Parent Teacher Association.

Williams, F., LaRose, R., & Frost, F. (1981). *Children, television and sex-role stereotyping.* New York: Praeger.

Williams. T.M. (Ed.). (1986). *The impact of television: A natural experiment in three communities.* New York: Academic Press.

Guides and Pamphlets for Helping Parents Teach Children About TV

1. *A Guide for Parents*

   Educational Improvement
      Center—South
   207 Delsea Drive
   R.D. 4, Box 209
   Sewell, NJ 08080

2. *Children and Televi-
   sion—A Primer for
   Parents*

   The Boys Town Center
   Boys Town, Nebraska 68010

3. *Parents' Television
   Guide*

   Richard P. Adler, Author
   Quaker Oats Co.
   Corporate Affairs Dept.
   Merchandise Mart Plaza
   Chicago, IL 60654

4. *Self-Regulating Guidelines for Children's Advertising*

   Children's Advertising
      Review Unit
   Better Business Bureau, Inc.
   845 Third Avenue
   New York, NY 10022

5. *Sex on Television*

   D.L. Green, Author
   Health Care of Southeastern
      Mass.
   (see below No. 7)

6. *The Family Learning
   Guide—Television*

   Family Learning
   19 Davis Drive
   Belmont, CA 94002

7. *The Prime-Time Primer*   Health Care of Southeastern
    Mass, Inc.
728 Brockton Avenue
Abington, MA 02351

8. *The Question of TV*   New Jersey Coalition for
    Viewing and Children   Better TV Viewing
P.O. Box 2381
Trenton, NJ 08607

9. *TV Impact on Television*   J.C. Penney Co., Inc.
Consumer Affairs Division
1301 Ave. of the Americas
New York, NY 10019

10. *What Parents Should*   Channing L. Bete Co., Inc.
    Know About TV   200 State Road
So. Deerfield, MA 01373

Activities

1. Choose one of the following activities:

   a. While watching a situation comedy, write down how many jokes that are followed by laughter did not seem funny enough to make viewers laugh aloud.

   b. If you were a TV producer and you wanted the viewers to dislike a character, what techniques could you use?

   c. If you were a camera operator for a commercial and you wanted the viewers to like a political candidate, what would you do?

2. Write a letter to a favorite star, or to his or her network, to tell them what you like or don't like about the program.

3. If you have seen a commercial that you think is unfair or fair, write a letter of complaint or praise to the FTC, the advertiser, the network, or Action for Children's Television.

4. If you think there are too many commercials on children's TV programs, write to your Congressman or Senator.

5. If there is a children's program that is scheduled at an unreasonable time, write to the station or network to request a change of schedule.

6. Write a review of a TV program. You might get some ideas from a television guide review.

7. Read the reviews of the programs scheduled for tomorrow and decide which programs you want to watch. Younger children can talk to their parents about their preferences.

8. Use a Program Rating Activity chart. It can be used to encourage children to evaluate the quality of programs that they watch. List programs viewed on one day. Rate each program on a 1–5 scale with 5 as the highest rating.

| a favorite program | liked it very much | liked it | didn't like it much | didn't like the program at all |

Draw faces like those above that show how much you liked or didn't like a program.

- Did you learn anything from the program? Yes _____ No _____

- If so, list one or more things you learned.

- Instead of watching this program, what could you do?

Sources for Television-Related Materials

A sampling of the wide variety of efforts that is being made to harness the educational potential of television is presented below.

Critical Viewing Skills Curricula

A series of curricula have been developed which are intended to help children better understand the behind-the-scenes aspects of television productions:

Critical Television Viewing Skills Curriculum (K–5)

Southwest Educational Development Laboratory
211 East 7th Street
Austin, TX 78701

The Television Criti-Kit (Middle School)

WNET/Thirteen
Critical Viewing Skills Project
356 West 56th Street
New York, N.Y. 10019

Far West Laboratory for Educational Research (High School Curriculum)

1855 Folsom Street
San Francisco, CA 94103

Getting the Most Out of Television

An elementary school curriculum with seven videotapes, teacher's manual, and student workbooks, developed at

The Yale University Family Television Research and Consultation Center
Psychology Department
Box 11A, Yale Station
New Haven, CT 06520

Reading Skills

Several programs have been instituted which provide teacher/parent guides and reading lessons based on scripts from television shows and classic movies:

CBS Reading Program

51 West 52nd Street
New York, N.Y. 10019

Channel: Critical Reading/TV Viewing Skills

Educational Activities, Inc.
Freeport, N.Y. 11520

Movie Scriptreader Program

Films Incorporated
Moviestrip Division
1144 Wilmette Avenue
Wilmette, IL 60091

The Television Reading Program

Capital Cities Communications, Inc.
4100 City Line Avenue
Philadelphia, PA 19131

Instructional Television

The Agency for Instructional Television, a consortium of 19 state and provincial agencies, assists education through the development of television programs which are designed to promote essential critical-reasoning and study skills. *The Appalachia Educational Laboratory of West Virginia* has developed guides to supplement television shows for preschoolers, such as *Mister Rogers' Neighborhood* and *Captain Kangaroo.*

Agency for Instructional Television

Box A
Bloomington, Ind. 47401

Appalachia Educational Laboratory, Inc.

Division of Early Childhood
Charleston, W. VA. 25325

Things to Watch for in Children's Advertising

1. Is the size of the product made clear?

2. If batteries are needed for a mechanical toy, is this stated?

3. If assembly of a toy is required, does the ad say so?

4. Is a child or adult shown doing something unsafe?

5. Are children shown using a product not intended for children?

6. Are children shown using a product in a way that the average child couldn't?

7. Does the ad suggest that a child will be superior to friends or more popular if he owns a given product?

8. Does the ad employ any demeaning or derogatory social stereotypes?

9. Does the ad suggest that an adult who buys a product for a child is better or more caring than one who does not?

10. Do program hosts or characters appear in commercials within their own programs?

11. In print publications, are the title characters of the publications used in ads within their own publications?

12. If fantasy elements are used, are they clearly "just pretend?"

13. In ads featuring "free prizes," is the premium offer clearly secondary?

14. Is a child-directed advertising appeal being used for vitamins or medications?

15. Is there anything misleading about the product's benefits?

Prepared by: Children's Advertising Review Unit, National Advertising Division, Council of Better Business Bureaus, Inc., 845 Third Avenue, New York, New York 10025 (212)745–1353

Parents' Guidelines: Television and Your Children

These guidelines were developed by the Illinois Office of Education, and have been endorsed by the PTA.

1. Start early to develop your child's good viewing habits.

2. Encourage planned viewing of specific programs instead of random viewing. Be physically active with little ones between planned programs.

3. Look for children's programs featuring young people in your child's peer group.

4. Make sure TV viewing is not used as a substitute for participating in other activities such as trips to zoos, museums, or the introduction of hobbies.

5. Open up discussion with your children on sensitive TV themes to offer them the opportunity to raise questions which may remain unanswered in the content of these programs.

6. Explain that TV advertising is being paid for by the makers of the product being shown and that famous people say nice things about products for money.

7. Balance reading and television activities. Children can "follow up" interesting TV programs by checking out the library books from which some of the programs are adapted and by pursuing additional stories by the authors of those specific books.

8. Help children develop a balanced viewing schedule of action, comedy, fine arts, fantasy, sports, etc.

9. If you do not have cable TV, arrange for a proper antenna or distribution system to bring in a signal from a public television station so children will have the chance to have alternative programming.

10. Point out positive examples which show how various ethnic and cultural groups all contribute to making a better society.

11. Show positive examples of women performing competently professionally and at home.

12. Write to local newspapers, local TV stations, networks, the FCC and/or advertisers about programs which include excessive violence.

Television Organizations, Agencies, & Networks

I. Organizations and Groups
Action for Children's Television, 20 University Road, Cambridge, MA 02138 (617-876-6620). National organization of parents and professionals, working to upgrade television for children to eliminate commercialism from children's TV. Membership, newsletter,

campaigns, research information, film library facilities.

Children's Advertising Review Unit, National Advertising Division, Council of Better Business Bureaus, Inc., 845 Third Avenue, New York, N.Y. 10022. Reviews and evaluates advertising directed to children under twelve years of age. Publishes their guidelines in a pamphlet for parents.

Museum of Broadcasting, 1 East 53rd Street, New York, New York 10022 (212) 752-4690. Maintains a collection of television programs on videotape and a reference library.

National Coalition on Television Violence, 1530 P Street, N.W., P.O. Box 12038, Washington D.C. 20005. Publishes a Newsletter.

II. Government Agencies

For letters about TV programs: Chairman, Federal Communications Commission, Washington, D.C. 20554

For letters about TV commercials: Chairman, Federal Trade Commission, Bureau of Consumer Protection, Washington, D.C. 20580.

To your Senator: U.S. Senate, Washington, D.C. 20515
To your Congressman: U.S. House of Representatives, Washington, D.C. 20515

III. TV Networks

ABC, 1330 Avenue of the Americas, New York, N.Y. 10019 (212) 887-7777

CBS, 51 West 52 Street, New York, N.Y. 10019 (212) 975-4321

NBC, 30 Rockefeller Plaza, New York, N.Y. 10112 (212) 664-4444

PBS, 1320 Braddock Place, Alexandria, VA 22314 (703) 739-5000

Chapter 1

A.C. Nielsen Co. *1988 Nielsen Report on Television*. Northbrook, Ill: Nielsen, 1988.

The Arbitron Company. 142 West 57 Street, New York, N.Y. 10019 (212) 877-1300.

Caldeira, J., J.L. Singer, and D.G. Singer. "Imaginary Playmates: Some Relationships to Preschoolers' Spontaneous Play, Language and Television-Viewing." Paper presented at the meeting of the Eastern Psychological Association, Washington, D.C., March 1978.

Collins, W.A. "Children's Comprehension of Television Content." In E. Wartella, ed., *Development of Children's Communicative Behavior*. Beverly Hills, Calif.: Sage, 1979, pp. 21–52.

Cook, T.D., H. Appleton, R.F. Conner, A. Shaffer, G. Tamkin, and S.J. Weber. *"Sesame Street" Revisited*. New York: Russell Sage Foundation, 1975.

Essa, E.L. "The Impact of Television on Mother-Child Interaction and Play" Doctoral dissertation, Utah State University, 1977. *Dissertation Abstracts International,* Vol. XXXIX (1978), 2568B (University Microfilms No. 78–21, 124).

Friedrich, L.K., and A.H. Stein. "Prosocial Television and Young Children: The Effects of Verbal Labeling and Role Playing on Learning and Behavior." *Child Development,* Vol. XLVI (1985), pp. 27–38.

Harrison, L.F. and T. MacBeth Williams. "Television and Cognitive Development" In T. MacBeth Williams, ed., *The Impact of Television: A National Experiment in Three Communities.* New York: Academic Press, 1986, pp. 87–142.

Hornik, R.C. "Television Access and the Slowing of Cognitive Growth." *American Educational Research Journal,* Vol. XV (1978), pp. 1–15.

Piaget, J. *Play, Dreams and Imitation in Childhood.* New York: Norton, 1962.

Singer, D.G., and T. Revenson. *A Piaget Primer: How a Child Thinks.* New York: International Universities Press and New American Library, 1978.

Singer, D.G., and J.L. Singer. "Family Television Viewing Habits and the Spontaneous Play of Preschool Children." *American Journal of Orthopsychiatry,* Vol. XLVI (1976), pp. 496–502.

Singer, D.G., and J.L. Singer. "Television Viewing and Aggressive Behavior in Preschool Children: A Field Study." *Annals of the New York Academy of Science,* Vol. CXLVII (1980), pp. 292–303.

Singer, D.G., D.M. Zuckerman, and J.L. Singer. "Teaching Elementary School Children Critical Television Viewing Skills: An Evaluation." *Journal of Communication,* Vol. XXX, No. 3 (1980), pp. 84–93.

Singer, J.L., and D.G. Singer. *Television, Imagination and Aggression: A Study of Preschoolers.* Hillsdale, N.J.: Erlbaum, 1981.

Susman, E.J. "Visual and Verbal Attributes of Television and Selective Attention in Preschool Children." *Developmental Psychology,* Vol. XIV (1978), pp. 565–566.

Tower, R.B., D.G. Singer, J.L. Singer, and A. Biggs. "Differential Effects of Television Programming on Preschoolers' Cognition, Imagination, and Social Play." *American Journal of Orthopsychiatry,* Vol. XLIX (1979), pp. 265–281.

Witelson, S.F. "Sex and the Single Hemisphere: Specialization of the Right Hemisphere for Spatial Processing." *Science,* Vol. CXCIII (1976), pp. 425–427.

Chapter 2

Bandura, A. *Aggression: A Social Learning Analysis.* Englewood Cliffs, N.J.: Prentice-Hall, 1973.

Huesmann, L.R., and L.D. Eron, eds. *Television and the Aggressive Child.* Hillsdale, N.J.: Erlbaum, 1986.

Singer, J.L., and D.G. Singer. "Family Experiences and Television Viewing as Predictors of Children's Imagination, Restlessness, and Aggression." *Journal of Social Issues,* Vol. XLII, No. 3, (1986), pp. 107–124.

Singer, J.L., D.G. Singer, and W. Rapaczynski. "Family Patterns and Television Viewing as Predictors of Children's Beliefs and Aggression." *Journal of Communication,* Vol. XXXIV, No. 2, (1984), pp. 73–89.

Zuckerman, D.M., D.G. Singer, and J.L. Singer. "Television Viewing and Children's Reading and Related Classroom Behavior." *Journal of Communication,* Vol. XXX, No. 1, (1980), pp. 166–174.

Zuckerman, D.M., D.G. Singer, and J.L. Singer. "Children's Television Viewing, Racial and Sex-Role Attitudes." *Journal of Applied Social Psychology,* Vol. X, No. 4, (1980), pp. 281–294.

Chapter 3

Singer, D.G. "Television and Children. How do You View?" *Child International*, Vol. I, No. 2, (1987), pp. 4–6.

Singer, D.G. "Television and Your Child." *Weekly Reader: To Parents*, Middletown, CT, Winter, 1987.

Singer, D.G., D.M. Zuckerman, and J.L. Singer. "Helping Elementary School Children Learn About TV." *Journal of Communication*, Vol. XXX, No. 3, (1981), pp. 84–93.

Singer, J.L., and D.G. Singer. *Television, Imagination and Aggression: A Study of Preschoolers.* Hillsdale, N.J.: Erlbaum, 1981.

Chapter 4

Alvarez, M., A.C. Huston, J.C. Wright, and D. Kerkman. "Gender Differences in Visual Attention to Television Form and Content." *Journal of Applied Developmental Psychology*, Vol. IX (1988), pp. 459–475.

Greenberg, B.S. "Minorities and the Mass Media." In J. Bryant and D. Zillmann, eds., *Perspectives on Mass Media Effects.* Hillsdale, N.J.: Erlbaum (1986), pp. 165–188.

Greenberg, B.S. "When Cable Television Comes Home." In S. Katz and P. Vesin, eds., *Children and the Media.* Los Angeles: Children's Institute International, (1985), pp. 71–76.

Huston, A.C., J.C. Wright, M.L. Rice, D. Kerkman, and M. St.Peters. "The Development of Television Viewing Patterns in Early Childhood: A Longitudinal Investigation." Paper presented at the International Communication Association Conference, May, 1989.

Mohr, P.J. "Parental Guidance of Children's Viewing of Evening Televison Programs." *Journal of Broadcasting*, XXIII (1979), pp. 213–228.

Pearl, D., L. Bouthilet, and J. Lazar (Eds.). *Television and Eehavior.* (DHHS Publication No. ADM 82–1195, Vol. 2). Washington, D.C.: U.S. Government Printing Office, 1982.

Postman, Neil. *Amusing Ourselves to Death.* New York: Viking, 1985.

Von Feilitzen, C. "The Functions Served by the Media: Report on a Swedish Study." In R. Brown, ed., *Children and Television.* Beverly Hills, Calif.: Sage, 1976.

Chapter 6

Field, M. *Good Company.* London: Longmans Green, 1952.

Huston, A., and J. Wright. "Children's Processing of Television. The Informative Functions of Formal Features." In J. Bryant and D.R. Anderson, eds., *Children's Understanding of Television. Research on Attention and Comprehension.* New York: Academic Press, 1983, pp. 35–68.

Salomon, G. "Internalization of film.. Schematic Operations in Interaction with Learners' Aptitudes." *Journal of Educational Psychology,* Vol. LXVI, (1974), pp. 499–511.

Chapter 7

Crane, Valerie. "Audience Response to *DeGrassi Junior High,* 'Best Laid Plans'." Research Communications, Ltd., Brookline, MA, 1987.

Friedrich, L.K., and A.H.Stein. "Aggressive and Prosocial Television Programs and the Natural Behavior of Preschool Children." *Monographs of the Society for Research in Child Development,* Vol. XXXVIII (1973), pp. 1–64.

Garry, R. "Television's Impact on the Child." In *Children on TV: Television's Impact on the Child.* Washington, D.C.: Association for Childhood International, 1967.

Greenfield, R., and J. Beagles-Roos. "Radio vs. Television: Their Cognitive Impact on Children of Different Socioeconomic and Ethnic Groups." *Journal of Communication,* Vol. XXXVIII, (1988) pp. 71–92.

Katz, E., and D. Foulkes. "On the Use of the Mass Media as 'Escape': Clarification of a Concept." *Public Opinion Quarterly,* Vol. XXVI (1962), pp. 377–388.

Murray, J.P., and K. Krendl. "Television and Fantasy: Children's Viewing and Storytelling." Unpublished manuscript, Department of Family and Child Development, Kansas State University, Manhattan, 1989.

Noble, G. *Children in Front of the Small Screen.* London: Constable, 1975.

Paulson, F.L. "Teaching Cooperation on Television: An Evaluation of 'Sesame Street' Social Goals Program." *AV Communication Review,* Vol. XXII (1974), pp. 229–246.

Piaget, J. *Play, Dreams and Imitation in Childhood.* New York: Norton, 1962.

Singer, D.G., and J.L.Singer. *Make Believe: Games and Activities to Foster Imaginative Play in Young Children.* Glenview, Ill.: Good Year Books, Scott, Foresman and Company, 1985.

Singer, J.L., and D.G. Singer. *Television, Imagination and Aggression: A Study of Preschoolers.* Hillsdale, N.J.: Erlbaum, 1981.

Snow, R.P. "How Children Interpret TV Violence in Play Contexts." *Journalism Quarterly,* Vol. LI (1974), pp. 13–21.

Tower, R., D.G. Singer, J.L. Singer, and A. Biggs. "Differential Effects of Television Programming on Preschoolers' Cognition and Play." *Journal of Orthopsychiatry,* Vol. XLIX, No. 2 (1979), pp. 265–281.

Williams, F., R. Larose,and F. Frost. *Children, Television and Sex-Role Stereotyping.* New York: Praeger, 1981.

Chapter 8

Edelbrock, C., and A.I. Sugawara. "Acquisition of Sex-Typed Preferences in Preschool-Aged Children." *Developmental Psychology,* Vol. XIV (1978), pp. 614–623.

Erikson, E. *Childhood and Society.* New York: Norton, 1963.

Friedrich, L.K., and A.H. Stein. "Aggressive and Prosocial Television Programs and the Natural Behavior of Preschool Children." *Monographs of the Society for Research on Child Development,* Vol. XXXVIII (1973), pp. 1–64.

Gorney, R., D. Loye, and G. Steele. "Impact of Dramatized Television Entertainment on Adult Males." *American Journal of Psychiatry,* Vol. CXXXIV (1977), pp. 170,174.

Wroblewski, R., and A.C. Huston. "Televised Occupational Stereotypes and their Effects on Early Adolescents: Are they Changing?" In D.G.Singer, and J.L.Singer, eds., *The Journal of Early Adolescence,* Vol. I, No. 3, (1987), pp. 283–297.

Chapter 9

Calvert, S.L., and A.C. Huston. "Television and Children's Gender Schemata." In L.Liben and M.Signorella, eds., *Children's Gender Schemata: Origins and Implications.* In the quarterly series. *New Directions in Child Development.* San Francisco: Jossey-Bass, (Winter, 1987), pp. 75–78.

Greenberg, B.S. "Minorities and the Mass Media." In J. Bryant and D. Zillman, eds., *Perspectives on Media Effects.* Hillsdale, N.J.: Erlbaum, (1986) pp. 165–188.

O'Bryant, S.L., and C.R. Corder-Bolz. "The Effects of Television on Children's Stereotyping of Woman's Work Roles." *Journal of Vocational Behavior,* Vol. XII (1978), pp. 233–244.

Williams, M., and J.Condry. "Living Color: Minority Portrayals and Cross-Racial Interactions on Televison." Paper presented at the meeting of the Society for Research in Child Development, Kansas, City, MO, 1989.

Zuckerman, D.M., D.G. Singer, and J.L. Singer. "Children's Television Viewing, Racial and Sex-Role Attitudes." *Journal of Applied Social Psychology,* Vol. X, No. 4, (1980), pp 281–294.

Chapter 10

Bandura, A. *Aggression: A Social Learning Analysis.* Englewood Cliffs, N.J.: Prentice-Hall, 1973.

Belson, W.A. *Television and the Adolescent Boy.* Hampshire, England: Saxon House, 1978.

Gerbner, G., L. Gross, M. Morgan, and N. Signorielli. "Living With Television: The Dynamics of the Cultivation Process." In J. Bryant and D. Zillman, eds., *Perspectives on Media Effects.* Hillsdale, N.J.: Erlbaum, (1986) pp. 17–40.

Huesmann, L.R., and L.D. Eron, eds., *Television and the Aggressive Child: A Cross-National Comparison.* Hillsdale, N.J.: Erlbaum, (1986).

Huesmann, L.R., L.D. Eron, M.M. Lefkowitz and L.O. Walder. "Stability of Aggression Over Time and Generations." *Developmental Psychology,* Vol. XX (1984), pp. 1120–1134.

Joy, L.A., M. Kimball, and M.L. Zabrack. "Television Exposure and Children's Aggressive Behavior." In T.M. Williams, ed., *The Impact of Television: A Natural Experiment Involving Three Towns.* Academic Press, New York, 1986.

Liebert, R.M., and J. Sprafkin. *The Early Window: Effects of Television on Children and Youth, 3rd edition.* New York: Pergamon, 1988.

Singer, J.L., and D.G. Singer. *Television, Imagination and Aggression: A Study of Preschoolers.* Hillsdale, N.J.: Erlbaum, 1981.

Chapter 11

Galst, J.P., and M.A. White. "The Unhealthy Persuader: The Reinforcing Value of Television and Children's Purchase-Influencing Attempts at the Supermarket." *Child Development,* Vol. XLVII (1976), pp. 1089–1096.

Goldberg, M.E., and G.J. Gorn. "Children's Reactions to Television Advertising: An Experimental Approach." *Consumer Research, Vol. I* (1974), pp. 69–75.

Iskoe, A. "Advertising via Famous Personalities and the Effects on Children." Unpublished manuscript, The Wharton School, University of Pennsylvania, 1976.

Kunkel, D.L. "A Survey of Nonprogram Content During Children's Programming on Independent Television Stations." Unpublished manuscript, University of California, Santa Barbara, 1987.

Liebert D.E., J.N. Sprafkin, R.M. Liebert, and E.A. Rubinstein. "Effects of Television Commercial Disclaimers on the Product Expectations of Children." *Journal of Communication,* Vol. XXVII, No. 1 (1977), pp. 118–124.

Shaak, B.. L. Annes, and J.R. Rossiter. "Effects of the Social Success Theme on Children's Product Preference." Paper presented at the Conference on Culture and Communications, Philadelphia, March 1975.

Ward, S., D.B. Wackman, and E. Wartella. *Children Learning to Buy: The Development of Consumer Information Processing Skills.* Beverly Hills, Calif.: Sage, 1976.

Index